RELIGION, POLITICS AND
THE MORAL LIFE

Selected Writings of Michael Oakeshott

General editors:

Shirley Robin Letwin
Timothy Fuller

Also available:

The Voice of Liberal Learning: Michael Oakeshott on Education
(introduced and edited by Timothy Fuller)

Morality and Politics in Modern Europe: The Harvard Lectures
(edited by Shirley Robin Letwin)

RELIGION, POLITICS AND THE MORAL LIFE

Michael Oakeshott

Edited by Timothy Fuller

YALE UNIVERSITY PRESS
NEW HAVEN AND LONDON 1993

Set in Linotron Baskerville by Best-set Typesetter Ltd.,
Hong Kong
Printed and bound in Great Britain by The Bath Press, Avon

Library of Congress Cataloging-in-Publication Data

Oakeshott, Michael Joseph, 1901–1990
    Religion, politics, and the moral life / Michael Oakeshott;
  edited by Timothy Fuller.
        p.   cm.
    Includes bibliographical references and index.
    ISBN 0-300-05643-5
    1. Religion and politics.   2. Religion and ethics.
  3. Political science – Philosophy.   I. Fuller, Timothy, 1940–   .
  II. Title.
  BL65.P7034   1993
  291.1'77 – dc20   93-1607
                                                              CIP

A catalogue record for this book is available from
The British Library

CONTENTS

Preface *by Timothy Fuller*   vii

Introduction *by Timothy Fuller*   1

1 Religion and the World   27

2 Religion and the Moral Life   39

3 Some Remarks on the Nature and Meaning of
   Sociality   46

4 The Importance of the Historical Element in   63
   Christianity

5 The Authority of the State   74

6 The Claims of Politics   91

7 Scientific Politics   97

8 The Customer is Never Wrong   111

9 The Concept of a Philosophy of Politics   119

10 Political Philosophy   138

Select Bibliography   156

Editor's Acknowledgements   159

Index   160

v

PREFACE

Timothy Fuller

Michael Oakeshott, we can now say, wrote a great deal of much interest that he never published.[1] In the 1920s and 1930s he wrote and did not publish as much as he wrote and did publish. This large unpublished cache comprises mostly fully elaborated, completed manuscripts, some handwritten, some typed. Most but not all of these Oakeshott dated. In the present volume, four of the essays have never before been published. Two of these four are typed and dated in his hand (1925 and 1929), and two are undated handwritten originals. Of the latter two, I judge that 'The Concept of a Philosophy of Politics' was written in the mid-1940s, around the time Oakeshott was producing his edition of Hobbes's *Leviathan*, and that 'Political Philosophy' was probably written a bit later, near the time he was composing 'Political Education'.

There are other essays and several book-length manuscripts.[2] These manuscripts reveal Oakeshott's early style and intellectual preoccupations, for at that time Oakeshott often spelt

[1] The most complete bibliography of Oakeshott's published works, taking account of all previous bibliographical work by W. H. Greenleaf, J. L. Auspitz, Oliver Starp and Paul Franco, has been published by John H. Liddington in *The Achievement of Michael Oakeshott*, edited by Jesse Norman (London: Gerald Duckworth and Co. Ltd, 1993).

[2] There is a typescript from the mid-1920s, about 190 pages in length, titled *A Discussion of Some Matters Preliminary to the Study of Political Philosophy*. A work of nearly the same length from the 1930s, without a general title, could, on the basis of its chapters, be called *The Politics of Faith and the Politics of Scepticism*, 'politics of faith' referring to what later Oakeshott called 'rationalism in politics', 'politics of scepticism' referring to Oakeshott's own idea of politics as the 'pursuit of intimations' that he developed in *Rationalism in Politics*. There are eight lectures, presented at Harvard in the late 1950s, called *Morality and Politics in Modern Europe*, in part a prototype for *On Human Conduct* (1975). Numerous notebooks from the 1920s of his own extensive commentaries on Plato's dialogues, Aristotle's *Nicomachean Ethics* and *Politics*, Spinoza's writings and those of others, include parallel quotations from commentators Oakeshott was reading at the time. There are occasional essays on the philosophy of history, on education and on law.

out in detail the authors and books he was reading, occasionally compiling lists of works consulted. The footnoted references in these cases are extensive by contrast to the published essays, and much more revealing of what interested him at that time. Oakeshott's reticence about discussing sources and influences is legendary among students of his work. Comparing the published and unpublished works, one finds that the published works achieve an idiomatic independence expressing his oft celebrated style and showing how deeply Oakeshott ingested and transformed the sources, making them his own. Yet the unpublished works are not drafts of the published works; they are different expressions of his ideas, often illuminating and accessible in a way that the more brilliant published works tend not to be for some readers.

The notebooks of the 1920s make it clear that he studied the works of Plato and Aristotle in considerable detail, often writing out line-by-line analyses of their major works. His comments on Plato's *Republic* could have been the basis for a substantial commentary. Nonetheless, he apparently did this solely for his own edification; there are no manuscripts on either Plato or Aristotle. He took a strong interest in Spinoza's writings, devoting almost as much space to him in his notebooks as to Plato and Aristotle, while Hobbes makes little explicit appearance at this stage.

INTRODUCTION

Timothy Fuller

Oakeshott's interest in religion and theology in the 1920s is pronounced. This is true of all of his essays of the period, published and unpublished. They both show the idiosyncratic nature of his religious outlook and express convictions about the living of one's life that describe the self-understanding he exhibited in the life he actually lived.

The previously unpublished essay 'Religion and the World' (1929) especially works out the point of view Oakeshott adopted for the conduct of his own life. It is his philosophical reflection on what it means to live 'religiously' in the 'world'. Philosophically, the essay, in common with many of the essays of the period, prefigures his argument that the human world is constituted as a world of thought, which he later elaborated in *Experience and its Modes* (Cambridge U.P., 1933).

Oakeshott remarks the tendency in Christianity from the beginning to dichotomize the world. In the primitive Church the dichotomy was understood to be between the present age and the redeemed age of the heavenly kingdom to come, which would supersede the present age. In medieval times, in the wake of the 'delay' of the eschaton, it was the dichotomy between the fleshly and the spiritual worlds. In post-medieval times the language of dichotomy between flesh and spirit was gradually transformed into a dichotomy between two scales of values within the world – one materialistic and vulgar, the other intellectual/spiritual and, one might say, 'noble', although Oakeshott shies away from high language. There is in this something, purged of grandeur and pretension, echoing Matthew Arnold, but filtered through Kierkegaard, Nietzsche and Pater, all of whom he read at that time.

The modern development of Christian thinking is what Oakeshott found both congenial as a catalyst for his thought, and, though in no sense a mere return, closer to the original experience of Christianity than the medieval alternative; it dramatizes the sense that human beings must choose how to live here and now, and what we choose will constitute our fundamental religious task.

In order to reach the modern idea emphasizing choice between two alternative modes of conducting a life on earth – wherein speculation on relating that choice to an afterlife recedes – it was necessary to overcome the medieval distinction between the 'natural' and the 'supernatural'. But all of these Christian ways of thinking Oakeshott treats as the historical unfolding of alternative interpretative responses to a divide understood as central in human experience. The vividness of the Christian experience resides in the constant effort of human beings to make sense of the world in terms of their belief that there are dichotomous alternatives and that a choice must be made. Unity of one's life, satisfaction within life, is a matter of gaining a self-understanding which is coherent for us, which promises to unify what is divided. The way, however, in which we characterize the fundamental choices, and conceive coherency, changes over time.

Oakeshott finds 'world' a term invested with many different meanings and no immutable meaning, although it has a number of historically identifiable focal meanings that can be recovered. Oakeshott distinguishes 'worldly' from 'religious' for the present age: the worldly man's world has a material character, a process with a past and future which, he believes, defines him and sets for him his task in life; it provides an external measure of success and bids him to measure himself by his achievement on its scale. Success as an external standard dominates. Career is central; safety, prudence, regularity and possession the desiderata.

By contrast, the 'religious man' seeks insight, sensibility, self-understanding; he bears concern for the features of the worldly life lightly and with a certain disdain. The issue for the religious man is to live according to what he understands and concludes to be of value, not taking what is offered from elsewhere as a true measure without critically judging it. The religious man is self-contained without demanding isolation or rejecting others. He aspires to be something for himself in the midst of a world which invites the abandonment of such effort: 'Ambition and the world's greed for visible results, in which each stage is a mere approach to the goal, would be superseded by a life which carried in each of its moments its whole meaning and value.' The religious man lives in the present moment and for the possibility of realizing himself then and there. He seeks to achieve a consistent character in the midst of the contingencies of life through the clarity of his vision of what he supposes he is and is trying to become. This means that to live religiously is not to live for the prevailing standards, nor for some career goal, but for gaining insight and sensibility, and with a commitment to enjoy 'candid detachment in the face of the very highest actual achievement'. In short, 'achievements' do not count much; what counts most is to conduct one's life in accordance with one's self-chosen understanding of the possibilities of life in the time and place one has. Achievements are but secondary manifestations of the lived life.

Religion is 'simply life itself, life dominated by the belief that its value is in the present'. To be always preparing for life as if it were yet to come, to be always acting now for the sake of some putative later repose, result or salvation is to lead an irreligious or worldly life. The religious individual lives between the extremes of moral prejudice and moral experiment: the former ties one to a hypothetical past perfection, the latter to a hypothetical perfection to come. Each conspires against the animating spirit of one's own self-understanding to be realized here and now. To live religiously is to live with freedom from regret for the past and from calculation for the future; both regret and calculation and invitations to a tedious round of imitation or loss of *self*-understanding. Oakeshott will take nothing in exchange for the self. He is content to be something for himself and cares not whether he is known to be something. This is his attitude and intention.

This is exactly the outlook Oakeshott carried with him throughout his life. It permeates all of his writing, even though often elusively or in a concealed way. I am not suggesting that he had anything like a secret or esoteric doctrine. It is true that after the early 1930s he wrote virtually nothing that overtly discussed these topics. Discerning readers note his references in later writings to biblical images, such as the Tower of Babel, and his meditation on religious experience in *On Human Conduct* (Oxford: Clarendon Press, 1975); but these are so brief as to be confusing to those who have concluded that Oakeshott was an irreligious thinker or an 'atheist'. It is true that he was disdainful of most religious declarations, as he was of much intellectual fashion generally. He was able to be quietly severe in his judgements but he was, on the other hand, tolerant and little inclined to be overtly judgemental. He knew well the difficulties of saying anything of value on the most important questions. For the same reason he was hard to please and quietly severe in his judgements. Oakeshott was severe on himself as well, and thus reticent when speaking on religious questions. I believe this is why many things he wrote he did not publish even though he clearly made them publishable. His reticence was his acknowledgement of the difficulties the human imagination must face in seeking to express itself religiously. He thought only a few had ever succeeded brilliantly in the undertaking, most notably St Augustine. For him, theologizing succeeded only if it could present an arresting construction of human experience as the encounter with the eternal in the midst of the irreparable temporality of our lives.

In the last few years of his life, we conversed often on these topics. His exegeses of classic theological writings were remarkable. It is our loss that he did not write them out. We can, however, construct a picture of his religious outlook on the basis of what he did write on these matters, episodic though it is.

In 'Religion and the Moral Life', presented first to his Cambridge colleagues at a meeting of the D Society,[1] Oakeshott rejects the idea that religion and morality are identical, pro-

[1] Published as a 'D Society Pamphlet' by Bowes & Bowes in 1927. The D Society was a group of around six Cambridge dons who met weekly in term-time to present theological papers to each other. Oakeshott wrote me a letter in 1988 describing the D Society as he knew it in the 1920s. John Liddington has kindly shown me a copy of a letter he obtained through Bikhu Parekh, written by Boys-Smith in 1939. Boys-Smith, a Cambridge theologian and one of Oakeshott's close friends, described the D Society. According to him, the 'D' had no significance. I remember asking Oakeshott what it meant: he never answered clearly. Oakeshott describes the participants as theological 'modernists'; Boys-Smith says their purpose was to study the 'Doctrine of the Church of England in the light of knowledge acquired since its formularies were compiled'. Dr John Sandwith Boys-Smith, former Vice-Chancellor of Cambridge University (1963–65) and Master of St John's College, Cambridge (1959–69), died in 1991. He was born on 8 January 1901 at Hordle, Hampshire where his father was the vicar. He was educated at Sherborne and St John's College, Cambridge. Initially he read economics but switched to theology. He was influenced by Rudolf Bultmann and the concept of 'demythologization' after studying in Marburg. Subsequently, he identified himself with the liberal modern churchmen of England. Ordained in 1926, Boys-Smith returned to Cambridge as Fellow and Chaplain of St John's, and served also as Director of Theological Studies. From 1931 to 1940 he was a university lecturer in theology. He was then elected to the Ely professorship which included becoming a canon of Ely Cathedral. He later went through a period of considerable doubt followed by a reaffirmation of personal faith. His writings include *Religious Thought in the 18th Century* (1934), and *Memories of St John's College* (1983).

posing instead that 'morality is a condition of religious belief', having to do with 'honesty with oneself'. 'Religion', he argued,

> if it is an activity of human beings must be the activity of moral personalities; and no religious doctrine or notion can properly be called 'religious' if it does not accord with the requirements of moral personality. . . . Since religion is a relation between God and moral persons, all notions of irresistible grace operating mechanically are impossible, for the characteristic of moral personality is its autonomy.

The moral and the religious, in short, are intertwined, and it is in our self-enactment that we succeed or fail in making them go together for us in our particular circumstances. It follows both that a religious community can never be fully articulated in abstract rules or catechetical exercises, and also that the boundaries between the 'Church' and the 'world' will always be uncertain and necessarily matters of interpretation; how we draw the boundaries will vary and depend a good deal on the moral imagination.

In the moral dimension as such, we will always face the ordeal of living up to one 'ought' after another; no success in one case guarantees success in the next; no success in one case precludes another case for which we may or may not find adequate responses. Moral life is an endless series.

'In religion,' Oakeshott says,

> we achieve goodness, not by becoming better, but by losing ourselves in God. For goodness is never achieved by becoming better: that is the self-contradiction of morality that always runs the risk of being self-defeating. Religion, then, is the completion of morality, not in the sense of a final end to an historical series, but as the concrete whole is the completion of all the abstractions analysis may discover in it. Religion is not the sanction of morality, but the whole of which morality is an aspect, and in which mere morality perishes, that is, is discovered as an abstraction.[2]

The connection to 'Religion and the World' will also be clear. Moral conduct is inherent to social life, but it is animated

---

[2] Compare Bernard Bosanquet, whose work Oakeshott was reading at the time: 'We construct our world as an interpretation which attempts to restore the unity which the real has lost by our making its diversity explicit.' *Logic*, II. ix. 1.

in the self-understandings of individuals who enact their lives within what they find to be the moral structure of social life. The reality of the religious experience emerges in the inter-section of moral conduct with the desire for goodness, but that complex experience cannot be reduced to morality alone.

Oakeshott thus concluded that independence of the moral personality is the condition of knowing dependence on God, where such dependence does not and cannot mean blindly obeying God's will. Dependence on God here means imagin-ative awareness of that which is not satisfied in moral conduct, but which cannot be ignored as a feature of our aspiration to understand ourselves fully. In blind obedience the moral van-ishes, excluding a defining characteristic of being human. Re-ligious experience is thus a profound occasion of self-awareness.

But, Oakeshott goes on, the formal autonomy of the moral personality has to be connected to a moral content: 'Free action is not moral action unless it is also wise. . . . A concrete moral action is the autonomous, free *and adequate* reaction of a personality to a situation.' The practical wisdom of our actions is not the achieving of goodness; the good is not an achieve-ment but a kind of transcending of the self that the self can imagine and experience as the losing of oneself in God, but which the self cannot simply bring about by wishing to do so. It is true that in this experience we are actively doing some-thing, but there is no policy that can be designed to bring about the desired fulfilment, if we can even state what that is supposed to be. From this perspective, religion cannot be the sanction of morality because religious experience is not a reward for moral conduct. To think that it is such a reward vulgarizes the religious experience. Here Oakeshott's view re-minds one of the examination of piety in Plato's *Euthyprho*.

The experience of transcendence is an encounter through sensibility and insight that occurs in the midst of the ordi-nariness of our diurnal context. Oakeshott treats the tran-scending experience neither as an excuse for immoderation nor as negating the necessity of moral deliberation and choice. Nor is Oakeshott prone to speak of transcendence as such. When speaking of what corresponds to it in his outlook, he never describes it as the intervention of the 'wholly other' into our realm of experience. We can only speak of such encounters in ways that situate them in our all too human experience. As we do not induce this encounter, Oakeshott also always speaks of it as the unanticipated, even if hoped-for, discovery of something intimated in what we are already doing.[3] There is little expression in his writings of struggle or anxious quest, and only infrequently does he dwell on mortality. When he does, he does so in a poetic mood. There is the sense of waiting for or letting the encounter happen. Bringing it about is not the object of moral conduct. Moral conduct, one could say, merely maintains relationships of human beings with each other as they continually shape and adjust their lives together. On the other hand, this maintenance and adjustment are marks of human accomplishment, sometimes of an extraordinary sort.

Morality cannot help but manifest itself in a history of the actual conduct of individuals even as it reveals the universal character of the human as the capacity to enter into moral relationships. Human beings must conduct themselves in specific actions, and, in conducting themselves, the religious element can shine through. We cannot be religious without enacting a pattern of moral practices; we cannot enact a pattern of moral practices without being moved, implictly or explicitly, by a desire for that completion in goodness which can never be captured fully in the particular decisions we take as we try to do what we think we ought to do. It should be noted, then, that Oakeshott's reference to completion or fulfilment in God is resolutely non-teleological. The religious experience for him separates us from nature – without becoming the 'supernatural' – in that it is entirely an implication of reflective consciousness; religious experience belongs entirely to being human.

Fulfilment is intimated in moral conduct but it is not to be attained by moral conduct. Yet we cannot speak of fulfilment without falling back on what we actually do as the imagining of what we think fulfilment might be. Thus, although at first it may seem Oakeshott is defining two separate dimensions of reality – that of transcending fulfilment and that of day-to-day response to contingent circumstances – he is actually describing different aspects of a single comprehensive range of imaginative human responses, which earlier he had called 'religious' and 'irreligious' or 'worldly'. We cannot speak about fulfilment or completion without expressing ourselves through accumulating historical experiences which cannot themselves

---

[3] Like Montaigne, Oakeshott thought that satisfaction comes by the way, incidentally, in the course of tending to our appointed business. The best results of one's engagements are discoveries, not constructions; they are concrete, specific, and only rarely achieved by calculation.

simply turn into the hoped-for fulfilment or completion. We make a duality out of a unity in the effort to make a unity we can never quite think we have finally come to possess. Oakeshott later reformulated Hobbes's ceaseless quest for power after power by transposing that insight into the language of the endless effort at self-understanding. By such transposition, Oakeshott sought to rescue the Hobbesian insight from the vulgar interpretations to which it is usually subjected.

There is an obvious connection between Oakeshott's religious view and his analysis of politics: in politics we construct visions of an order that are all too easily construed as the undistorted or true forms of 'defective' actually existing arrangements. In politics we understand ourselves to be situated between the way we think things are and the way we think they ought to be. We continually break the unity of our world of experience into the 'is' and the 'ought to be' in search of a unity that eludes us. The single realm of human experience continually tries to duplicate itself in a putatively better alternative. Politics is an undertaking that is vulnerable to the desire for perfection but incapable of achieving it. The Tower of Babel is the true story of the human condition at every moment.

For Oakeshott, then, a satisfactory understanding of religious experience would help us come to a clearer idea of political experience, assisting us to acknowledge that politics is, as he later argued in 'Political Education' (1951), a 'necessary evil'.[4] Political engagements are 'necessary' because they are both unavoidable and unsought (but Oakeshott does not call them 'natural' because their necessity does not determine their character); they are 'evil' because they too easily obscure our awareness that political aspirations cannot replace the fulfilment that comes in religious insight and individually cultivated sensibility, and thus detract from our capacity to live in the present. The 'worldly man' repeatedly politicizes this fulfilment and thus, intentionally or not, depreciates the present for the sake of a future present that we will not possess.

This temptation is summarized and rejected succinctly in Oakeshott's brief essay on 'The Claims of Politics' (*Scrutiny*, 8, 1939, pp. 146–51).[5] This essay also marks a move toward

[4] Published originally by Bowes & Bowes in 1951, reprinted in *Rationalism in Politics* (Methuen, 1962).

[5] 'The Claims of Politics' should be seen as accompaniment to Oakeshott's sceptical examination of the *Social and Political Doctrines of Contemporary Europe*, also published in 1939.

the increasing concern with politics that was to characterize Oakeshott's post-World War II writings. Oakeshott reminds us that to maintain and to rejuvenate a culture is not the task solely or principally of those who engage in public life:

> Just as the similar belief that the true, unhindered service of God was possible only to members of a religious order or officials of the Church (that is, to those who made a profession of it) promoted a false and irreligious division between those who were called to serve God and those who were not, and gave a false importance to the former, so this belief about social service promotes the erroneous view that some activity is disconnected from the communal life of a society and gives a false importance to the activity of those who engage in public life.

Oakeshott's post-Hobbesian/Lockean reformation theology informs his understanding of politics as well. Just as he rejects the distinction between the priest and the layman, so he rejects pejorative distinctions between public service and private selfishness. Social life is a whole composed of distinct and real individual members. The character of the social whole is in the care of, and dependent upon, the imagination of all its participants. Political responsibility is but one aspect of a larger whole which can never be understood adequately from the political viewpoint alone – perhaps not even primarily:

> A political system is primarily for the protection and occasional modification of a recognized legal and social order It is not self-explanatory; its end and meaning lie beyond itself in the social whole to which it belongs, a social whole already determined by law and custom and tradition, none of which is the creation of political activity.

Political engagements presuppose a civilization and are reactive to it. Those drawn to political involvement have their own, for Oakeshott often vulgar, motives. These are not generalizable as universal motives of human beings. Politics is necessary but to be kept in perspective and in its place. Politics maintains and defends social life (later, in 'Political Education', Oakeshott will say politics is the activity of 'attending' to society's arrangements), but seldom rejuvenates or recreates it. The latter task falls to poets, artists, philosophers and to the imaginative use of their resources by countless individuals.

The refreshment emanating from the poets, artists and philosophers requires them precisely not to be of the political world. Implicitly, then, Oakeshott distinguishes the mundane and vulgar from the poetic and reflective (the 'worldly' distinguished from the 'religious'), and politics is necessary but irrevocably mundane.[6]

Earlier, in his unpublished essay 'Some Remarks on the Nature and Meaning of Sociality' (1925), Oakeshott had argued both against postulating a social good superior to the individual, and also against postulating an individual whose good depends on resisting implication in the social whole. Oakeshott was an individualist, but not an abstract individualist. Individuality is a self-understanding composed in responding to others. We understand ourselves to be individuals because we are self-conscious within a context of innumerable self-conscious agents. Sociality is not, then, a simple division between oneself and the rest. The self is not a body in isolation, but a consciousness expressing itself as a participant in a community of discourse. Sociality is not mere 'sociableness' or 'gregariousness', and is not the opposite of solitude. Indeed, solitude is a condition in which sociality as Oakeshott understands it can be fully realized. Sociality is, he says, an 'intense union' that is not mere 'cohabitation'; it is a relation of moral beings not of bodies in proximity. To be merely physically in the presence of others is not only not sociality, it may be a real barrier to sociality.

In that essay, Oakeshott interprets Plato's 'justice', Aristotle's 'friendship', St Paul's 'caritas', each as designating the idea of unity as an intellectual/emotional achievement revealed in a common understanding that nonetheless preserves discernible individuality among those who make this unity. Discourse at once binds and distinguishes us, spawns a sense of both difference and familiarity. Politics sets certain background elements of the calculation of the distance to be maintained among those who are both at one and individual, but a profound sense of relatedness is attained in ways beyond the scope of any politics to comprehend or to direct. As Aristotle maintained, friendship transcends without denying legality. Sociality is, then, a mutual exploration – sometimes in closer, sometimes in more distant, relation – without a predetermined end that will terminate our efforts to understand ourselves in relation to each other. What

---

[6] One might note that Oakeshott, unlike Leo Strauss or especially Hannah Arendt, does not locate the heroic in the political realm. Transcendence is elsewhere.

Oakeshott describes is not a single-minded direction or purpose that enfolds us all, but rather a shared attitude towards
how to travel companionably together. This theme is to be
worked out magisterially, of course, only in *On Human Conduct*
(1975).

This is the heart of what may be called Oakeshott's Augustinianism: he has reinterpreted the doctrine of the two cities
so as to undermine the dualistic language of the traditional
Augustinian formulations, interrelating struggle and release in
never-ending human tales. I shall come back to this transposed
Augustinianism shortly.

Further evidence of the connection between his political
thinking and his conviction of the centrality of the human task
as self-understanding, lies in his 1928 essay, 'Authority of the
State'.

In 'Authority and the State', as was the case in 'Religion
and the World', Oakeshott questions the assumptions people
bring to the use of the terms 'authority' and 'state'. Almost
always definitions of such terms are abstractions in which some
one or a few features of what is involved are emphasized at the
expense of the full array of features that the term captures. To
understand authority depends on first seeing that a person is a
self-understanding enmeshed in relationships with others who
are their own self-understandings. Each is a responsive participant in an array of conditions of understanding already
existing, generated by all involved, past and present, and
within which each of us adopts an outlook. Individuals are
inevitably in relation, not cut off; but understanding cannot
live apart from the individually located insights of individuals
who intersect and overlap. Individuals engage in continual
mutual efforts to make themselves understood producing the
common conditions of our lives. But we are 'in common' as
each of us understands and appropriates the common for ourselves. The key to continuity and persistence of social life is
this continuous activity of contiguous and contingent interpretation and response.

Oakeshott concludes that authority exists in an individual's
accepting that something proposed is more than a matter of
mere preference, as something 'absolute, irresponsible [not ac-
countable to another], self-supporting and inescapable'. What
binds one is one's own sense that a proposal, an argument or a
rule is a necessary and satisfactory part of the whole that is
one's self-understanding. Even when we say that we accept

something because it emanates from one whom we acknowledge as 'having authority', the 'having authority' is attributed by us in our act of acknowledging. Imposition by force or threat cannot be authoritative. The claim of someone to have authority over us is validated by our assent. Nothing can 'cause' authority or an authoritative relationship to exist. Acknowledging the presence of something authoritative is our own conclusion through reasoning and responding.[7] What directs each of us is our own world of ideas in the form we find coherent and satisfactory for us. Authority is not an external cause (relationships of authority are moral relationships and thus matters of reciprocal recognition), but internal assent to a way of looking at things. It is a moral relationship because it is a self-imposed restraint.

The 'state' is 'the social whole which is correlative to individuals who are complete and living persons . . . the totality in an actual community which satisfies the whole mind of the individuals who comprise it'. Thus, for Oakeshott, the 'state', as he was then using the term, is not identical to the government or to the legal system or to any other subcategory of the totality of relationships among a set of individuals. The 'state' is the totality of the goings-on that is never fully revealed by reference to any of the particulars, individual or institutional, that make it up. Coercive power is subordinate to it. What turns coercion into a relationship of authority is the discovery of a satisfactory fit between a proposal and its acceptance.[8]

This 'state' is not animated by a unifying, directive purpose. To attribute to this whole a defining purpose we would be forced to abstract an element or elements within it, making them stand for the whole. No single purpose could ever define what 'state' is in Oakeshott's sense. A substitute for the whole is not the whole. Political purposes and ideological aspirations will always fall short of the whole. The whole is the comprehensive condition composing purposes, aspirations and policies that crystallize as active responses to, or attempts to control, the whole or reduce it to a putatively manageable

[7] The further development of Oakeshott's concept of political authority is found in the second essay of *On Human Conduct* and in 'The Rule of Law' in *On History and Other Essays* (1983).

[8] In Oakeshott's later writing 'state' recedes in favour of 'civil association' as his central expression for characterizing the 'modern European state'. This early, peculiar use of 'state' is intended to counteract a great deal of what is usually said about the state, particularly definitions emphasizing its coercive features or its comprehensive powers of control. But Oakeshott later came to consider it misleading language for expressing his view.

perspective. The 'state' is not a 'government' or a 'power'; nor is it a 'society' with an exhaustible list of identifying characteristics. It is the conditions of satisfaction for a set of people; thus it must include the purposes of all its members without being identified with any particular ones of them. Governments, churches, industries, armies are all organizational features within a whole that we fall back on in trying to make the state more obvious and understandable for ourselves than its full comprehensiveness can ever be.

At the same time, Oakeshott insists that the state is only its members in all of their relations with each other. The 'state' is not a mystery detached as an entity unto itself, but it is the sum total of conditions which insure that 'no government, as such, was ever strictly a sovereign power, or ever had more than a derivative "authority"'. Government cannot compel belief even if it can coerce behavior.[9]

Where does that conviction, that we should consent to the conditions of a 'state', come from? It comes from our constant effort to order ourselves in the world. The consent is acknowledgement of what is authoritative for us. It is quite remarkable that Oakeshott ends this essay quoting the frontispiece to the *Leviathan*: '*Non est potestas super terram quae comparetur ei*', 'No power on earth can be compared to him.' But for Oakeshott this means Hobbes's sovereign depersonalized, contingent, subdued. It allows us to see Oakeshott's argument as to why government and authority are indispensable, why they are fundamentally limited in what they can do and why the dis crepancy between aspiration and achievement is inevitable: the constituted 'authorities' never articulate all that needs articulation, and the subjects of authority cannot abandon their own understanding of what is meant and what they are to do or not to do.

This Augustinian/Hobbesian convergence connects Oakeshott's formulation of the Christian experience to the emerging features of his political philosophy. We can see this from a somewhat different angle in his 1928 essay on 'The Importance of the Historical Element in Christianity'. The emphasis in

---

[9] This is a foretaste of Oakeshott's later arguments on the idea of law and of civil association: We do not *obey* laws, he will later say, but 'subscribe' to them. We take them as qualifying conditions in choosing our courses of action. A law will not tell us not to light fires, for instance, but rather that we should not light fires arsonically. See 'The Rule of Law' in *On History and Other Essays* (Oxford: Basil Blackwell, 1983) and the second essay in *On Human Conduct* (Oxford: Clarendon, 1975).

that essay is on the radical temporality of the human condition. Oakeshott does not, however, identify the modern
historical outlook as such with the temporal (and mortal)
character of existence. Temporality of existence is fundamental
for human beings. The modern intellectual dominance of
the critical historian's outlook is a particular interpretative
response to the experience of temporality.

What Oakeshott is thinking of and criticizing, in referring to
the 'historical element', is the modern scholar's passion to
recover the 'original' Christian experience as if it could define
once and for all the essence of what it is to be Christian. He
thinks this quest for an originating and defining complex of
Christian experiences is but one of the ways, and a peculiarly
modern way, of trying to understand Christianity. And he sees
no reason to accept its prominence as final. He contrasts it
with the alternative experience of the immediacy of what he
calls 'the object of belief', an experience pragmatically grounded
in the 'ordinary wants of ordinary people'. For Oakeshott
personally sympathized, in religious matters, with the simple,
direct and immediate against the sophisticated, detached and
intellectual. In this sense, he is theologizing against theology
and against complex credal and doctrinal propositions.

Oakeshott denies that we can identify the original, whole
Christian experience. He does not think historians will be able
to tease out such an object of historical knowledge. Nor does he
think this is what religious experience is really about. Religious
events, like all others, are moments of noticeable, and temporary, coagulation in a relentless process of change and development. There is no fixed historical point that is separable
from its antecedents and consequents.

Indeed, nothing whatever can be identified in a fixed and
final fashion. We have to participate in the determination or
designation of the objects of our attention; such objects do not
present themselves to us independently, and could never do so
because they do not exist in that way. It is outside the realm of
possibility for a human being to be confronted by isolated
'facts as such'.[10] We must act to identify what we consider
objects of our concern. The religious response, therefore, can-

[10] At the time of these essays, Oakeshott did not employ the term 'facts' in as
unequivocal a fashion as he was later to do in his essays on history. It is clear,
however, that 'facts' always meant to him conclusions we had reached about what
we find we must treat as facts in our deliberations even though there is always the
possibility we would have to revise our view of the 'facts'. Facts are what we find no
way to get around so far.

not be to a fixed and final object of belief; we must instead come to a decision as to what we shall treat as the orienting object, and how by our response we shall characterize its meaning for us. Inevitably, this is central to self-understanding.

Nor is there any 'core' to be extracted from the original complex of Christian experiences. Oakeshott may have been thinking in 1928 of Bultmann's effort to separate kerygma from myth, and perhaps Catholic sacramentalism. For Oakeshott there is no such thing as a minimally necessary Christian 'essence' to which are attached adventitious historically changing accidents that leave the core untouched. Distinctions between core and accidents cannot be stabilized. We participate in the construction of meaning in determining as objects that to which we subsequently intend to refer.

As Oakeshott refuses to exempt anything from change, he takes up the question, what can we possibly mean by the 'identity' of Christianity? The identity, he says, is to be found 'in the facts of history, not as something unchanging, or some substance common to them all, but as a kind of qualitative sameness'. Christianity is a tradition that hangs together by persisting in its identity while constantly changing. As Oakeshott sees it,

> On this view of identity . . . the characteristic of being Christian may properly be claimed by any doctrine, idea or practice which, no matter whence it came, has been or can be drawn into the general body of the Christian tradition without altogether disturbing its unity or breaking down its consistency. This means that an idea or practice may properly be Christian which, in part at least, runs counter to much that had previously been regarded as Christian.

Oakeshott emphasizes the conventionality or civil character of religion. Thus what would be 'altogether' disturbing in appearing to depart too far from established religious practice is always going to be a matter of argument. If the distinctiveness of Christianity resides in its tradition taken comprehensively, its distinctiveness must be evident to, and manifested by, its practitioners in what they do and say. The tradition cannot be reduced to a core or to a set of propositions.[11]

[11] Readers who examine Oakeshott's work as a whole will, I think, see a connection between his treatment of Christianity as a tradition – and thus not an 'ideology' – and his rejection of 'rationalism' in politics. Consider in particular 'The Tower of Babel' (1948), in *Rationalism in Politics*.

There is a disposition among political philosophers who operate in the context of reformed Christianity going back at least to Hobbes and Locke, to simplify the requirements of belief that identify the Christian. For both Hobbes and Locke, for example, this became reliance on the simple proposition that 'Jesus is the Saviour.' All else is a matter of developing conventional practices within Christian congregations or Christian polities through time from the primitive Church onwards. But Oakeshott does not explicitly invoke even that basic proposition. In fact, he studiously avoids propositional language. Instead, he suggests that religion represents 'the highest' that people can believe and the 'best they can desire', reminiscent of the desire for completeness in 'Religion and the Moral Life'. Oakeshott sidesteps truth claims for religious beliefs. He spends no time analysing traditional theological doctrines, and he engages in no apologetics. Is this a philosopher's clinical detachment from religion, or is it Oakeshott's way of expressing the serenity of faith in the midst of an inconsequential world of incessant and unwinnable debate? There are suggestions in his writings to support either view.

Christianity's success or failure, Oakeshott concludes, depends on its capacity to maintain an identity while offering the highest expression for whatever historical age in which it is operating. Changing with the times is, he argues, what keeps religion relevant. The traditional symbols will remain, but they cannot abide for him solely in the authority of a teaching Church or hierarchy, but must come alive in their daily use. Christianity has persisted even if there are no fixed criteria by which to discriminate between orthodoxy and heresy; this is an irrelevancy in Oakeshott's descriptive scheme, even if it is felt to be of obvious practical import by many religious practitioners.

In order to persist, Christianity continually will admit the new and discard the old so long as there is no 'absolute break'. Yet Oakeshott gives no clear indication of what an absolute break would be since he presents no propositions of belief essential for a Christian to profess. Presumably in practice he expects the weight of tradition to have a powerful effect on such decisions. In light of his later arguments designed to demolish the pretensions of revolutionary ideologues in his essay 'Political Education', one might think that he doubts the possibility of anything that could qualify as an absolute break in the temporal succession of human events. Can there be any absolute breaks in the seamless web of historical change? This is a question that all students of Oakeshott's work must ponder, and one that is brought into sharp relief here. And if there can be no breaks in the seamless web, then the meaning of such things as the Incarnation must be reconsidered. Is everything, perhaps, incarnation?

One might look at the issue also in light of Oakeshott's repeated insistence in the 1920s that religion is fundamentally pragmatic. Religious ideas, he argues, do not depend 'entirely' on 'a demonstration of their ultimate truth'. But one wonders what the word 'entirely' means in this context. It is not clear that Oakeshott admits that religious ideas depend *at all* on a demonstration of their truth. Since religion and the religious consciousness 'are essentially practical', the adequacy of religion depends on its ability to satisfy 'the demands of ordinary life of ordinary people'. Religion begins in and with our simple wants and is not primarily a quest for knowledge or sophistication. Religious achievement is tied to 'an almost sensible perception of the reality of the object of belief' and works for us when we are 'made intensely aware of the actural existence of the object of belief'. Necessary truths have little or nothing to do with faith. Necessary truths do not require faith but rather acknowledgement or recognition. In order for this immediacy to occur, Oakeshott says that not truth but 'idolatry' is necessary. I presume he means by this that the religious consciousness must fulfil itself, practically speaking, in visible, material ways and cannot remain at the level of intellectual abstraction It was the simple devotion of the peasant in the field, or going to see Little Gidding, or coming upon a wisp of wheat on a wayside calvary that moved him, not theological treatises.

Insofar as Oakeshott alludes to Christ, he refers abstractly to the Founder and remarks that this focal point ensures that there will always be an historical element in Christianity but that it is also potentially always an historical abstraction that can block the immediacy of the religious experience. Christianity thus constitutes itself, for Oakeshott, in a dialectic between the historical and the immediate. But the immediate, we must remember, is itself a form of (perhaps unsophisticated) reflection, a way of understanding. The immediate is not merely immediate.

In any event, Christianity cannot dispense with either element, and this constitutes the characteristic Christian tension. Christianity is, one might speculate, a fundamental expression of the human condition in general, when that condition is understood as the incessant tension between preservation and change that, for Oakeshott, is our basic situation. Is Christianity, then, a way of expressing the universality of the human condition? If so, this might certify its distinctive significance while downplaying its imperial claims in terms of dogma and liturgical practice in favour of simple openness to the potential that lurks in all of human experience altogether.

But another dimension of this is hinted at in Oakeshott's unelaborated distinction between 'idolatry' and the authentic religious experience. These cannot be the same for him and yet they are somehow inextricably wedded to each other. Through reflectiveness we rise to the distinction between idolatry or, as I would put it, conventional religious expression, and the encounter with the eternal that may be initially expressed conventionally. But in rising to this distinction we do not transport ourselves from the world of human experience to some other world – we have no access to another world. The distinction is the result of critical reflection within the one dimension of human intelligence that we must inhabit. The temporal and the eternal are one and the same realm of human experience expressed in differing idioms.

This critical reflection leads to emphasis on the historical significance of Christianity and to consider what might be unchanging in the midst of the changing. As we have seen, this cannot be brought to completion because we cannot divest ourselves of the awareness, within critical historical reflection itself, that *we* are doing the work of identifying what we propose to call unchanging. How we identify the unchanging is itself changing, and must forever be so. Hence the historical consciousness can, so to speak, only temporarily cure the sickness of duality it itself produces.

Another response would be through ritual and sacrament. Here we understand the past to be rendered immediately present to us. But critical analysis breaks through here too when we attempt to explain, rationalize or define ritual and sacrament. Here the critical intelligence may dualize its experience, if only to end by reaffirming the mysteriousness of what it seeks to explain. The abatement of mystery is not an alternative to mystery, but is rather an acknowledgement of mystery even in the act of trying to make it less mysterious. It might be best to say that for Oakeshott there can be a sacramental attitude, but no objective sacraments. Revelation has to be a form of self-understanding if it is to carry authority for one's life. As we have seen, the absolute dependence upon God is to be reached through the experience of the absolute dependence upon our own capacity to understand.

If revelation must be for us as a kind of self-understanding, then Oakeshott can – again adapting Hobbes's sceptical analysis of claims to authority on the basis of private revelation – both affirm the universal possibility of revelation and, at the same time, seek to deprive it of (or protect it from) its potential use in fomenting disruption.

To put the issues yet another way, neither historical 'purity' (the effort to isolate the core meaning) nor historical scholarship are independently necessary, and either can pose a barrier to the religious experience. Historical purity can repress the creativity of the religious imagination, and arrest the adjustment to altered circumstances; historical scholarship can undermine the immediacy of religious experience. Each in its own way will distort in the effort to clarify.

We must also notice that Oakeshott has no interest in advancing the philosophical pursuit of truth at the expense of the religious pursuit of meaning. Nevertheless, he clearly separates them from each other. Philosophy he designates as the search for truth. Later, in *Experience and its Modes*, he argued that truth refers to the making coherent of our experience. It is what we seek in order to relieve the dissatisfying incoherence that besets consciousness. But philosophy for Oakeshott is also, categorically speaking, impractical. The search for truth has nothing to do with daily life. The desire for meaning or reconciliation has by contrast everything to do with daily life. Religion is preeminently practical. Yet its practicality has here no ordinary sense. It is the intimation of the completion of the endless tasks of daily life and the consolation for their interminability. The two forms of sought-after satisfaction, philosophical and religious, differ by reason of the two different conceptions of the experience of dissatisfaction to which they respectively respond.

In my view, Oakeshott is following the inspiration of Hobbes in insisting upon the separation of Christianity from all dependence on Aristotelian/scholastic teleology. I think he believed that Christianity thus purged was far closer to expressing the truth of the human condition than anything derived from teleological philosophy/theology. This position was not unique to Hobbes, but Oakeshott's long-standing fascination with Hobbes, and indeed his unusual interpretation of Hobbes in such essays as 'Leviathan: A Myth' (1947),[12] indicates that he absorbed Hobbes's theology far more thoroughly than is revealed in what he published.

I think Oakeshott concluded that teleological views are necessarily anti-Christian because, as he saw them, they emphasize knowledge rather than faith. Moreover, when amalgamated to Christian ideas, they force a dualism upon Christian thought – distinguishing the natural from the supernatural – that Oakeshott opposed in all facets of his thinking on every topic, religious or other, from start to finish. Anyone who would take the trouble to examine fully Hobbes's idea of Christianity as presented in *Leviathan* would, I believe, see the point.

To see the point one must examine Hobbes's rejection of the *summum bonum* in a different perspective from that taken by virturally all commentators. Let us recall that in *Leviathan*, chapter 11, Hobbes denied that anyone can enjoy 'the repose of a mind satisfied', as was spoken of 'by the old moral philosophers'. In the perspective of Hobbes's theology, the repose of a mind satisfied can come only with eternal life at the general resurrection. While the natural condition, which we must still endure in the interim between the first and Second Coming of Christ, prevails, what counts is the inner certainty of the Christian's faith that displaces the pursuit of the so-called 'highest good' as beside the point. The Second Coming is guaranteed by faith; there is nothing in the interim period we can do except prepare ourselves through personal strengthening; we can neither impede nor advance the historical end of things. It will come, but we can neither induce nor prevent it. The parallel for politics is clear: pursuing the 'highest good', under the natural conditions of mankind, will encourage both Pelagianism and anti-nomianism: Pelagianism, because we are misled into thinking that we can will the human condition to completion – but we cannot; anti-nomianism, because we are easily misled into thinking there must be a 'true' or 'correct' political order, accessible to our understanding, which is distorted or suppressed by the actually prevailing order.

From this perspective, a perspective that requires us to interpret Part I of *Leviathan* by taking seriously Parts III and IV, refusal to make the *summum bonum* our object, and hence an

---

[12] First published as 'The "collective dream of civilization"', *Listener* 37 (1947), pp. 966–67. Reprinted in *Hobbes On Civil Association* (Berkeley & Los Angeles: U. of California Press, 1975), pp. 150–54, as 'Leviathan: A Myth'.

object of contention, is a fundamentally Christian thing to do. It is so because it is the indication that our attention is fixed on our participation in a divine drama dependent on interpretative response and not on our location in the world of natural processes. It will not look that way to one whose Christianity is informed by what Hobbes calls Aristotelity.[13]

In rejecting the *summum bonum* one disposes the issue of coordinating the natural and supernatural ends – central to the scholastic tradition – which, in practice, encourages endlessly conflicting claims of authority under virtually all historical conditions. For Oakeshott (as for Hobbes), to reject the *summum bonum* is to begin to appreciate fully what the life of *faith* really is. The transformative power of Christian faith does not entail a radical transformation of the world as it now is, but rather induces a radical transformation in our understanding of the significance, or insignificance, of the present world.

Oakeshott emphasizes that answering the question about how we ought to live does not lie in postulating an ideal type of human being, there being no such type; it lies, rather, in elaborating the conditions to be observed by everyone in their conduct. Observance of proper conduct is the best practical manifestation of the Christian spirit, a spirit which is not distracted by overestimating the value of works in the world. The true Christian with inner, invisible faith does not need to be equipped with a substantive doctrine of what is best; it will suffice to know what the canons of good conduct towards other human beings are, summarized in the golden rule, and affirmed in the act of authorizing the sovereign to make the laws of the land. It is not from the aspiration to salvation that we deduce specific requirements of conduct here and now. Salvation is not a task to be performed, but an understanding to be worked out. Oakeshott's religious question is constituted in this task he thought of as self-understanding. It is a question which can neither be answered once and for all nor set aside. Augustine understood this. Hobbes posed the question thus: why, he asked (*Leviathan*, chapter 44), is there 'such diversity of ways in running to the same mark, *felicity*, if it be not night amongst us'? This is Oakeshott's question too, and a unifying theme in

[13] Hobbes says, in the Lutheran way, in *Leviathan* (chapter 43), that 'faith only justifies'. We cannot, he thinks, be saved by works because we are all sinners. Every action in this world is tainted by this fact about us. What conduces to our salvation is the will to conduct ourselves rightly which can only imperfectly manifest itself in our actions.

his work. In everything he wrote, he considered this fundamentally Christian question.

The post-World War II essays show Oakeshott's increasingly focused application of his thinking to the political situation of our time and to the task of defining for himself what it is to philosophize on politics. In 'Scientific Politics' (1947), for instance, Oakeshott reviewed favourably the conclusions, if not always the arguments, of Hans Morgenthau in his influential *Scientific Man Versus Power Politics*. He applauds Morgenthau's appreciation of the 'sporadic and uncertain' character of political success in an age when unfulfillable promises of such success have been continually made, and thus have been inevitably broken.

This is the 'great illusion of modern politics' which Oakeshott elucidated in his own 1947 essay, 'Rationalism in Politics', remedying what he considered Morgenthau's failure adequately to narrate the historical pedigree of 'rationalism' and 'scientism'. Oakeshott agrees with Morgenthau that the triumphs of modern natural science have intimidated those who were justly suspicious of the prospect of a science of society that would transform political conflicts into soluble, technical issues. For Oakeshott, this was not the fault of modern science, but the fault of those who, not themselves scientists, thought they could grasp and easily apply science to other modes of human experience.

As we have seen earlier, for Oakeshott human existence cannot be reduced merely to a series of technical problems to be solved. Political problems are not scientific problems. The word 'problem' enjoys no universal meaning unless by misplaced fiat. Oakeshott and Morgenthau each express the Augustinian, anti-Pelagian stance. If there is anything to be called a 'science of politics', it has to do with limiting and dispersing power for the sake of the social whole as Oakeshott had earlier defined it.

Thus also in 1955 in 'The Customer Is Never Wrong' he dissented from Walter Lippmann's call for a 'public philosophy', which, while avoiding mere ideology, nevertheless displayed that powerful strain in American politics that seeks a directive vision and guide that, to use the terms of Oakeshott's earliest writing, constitute 'worldliness' or lack of faith. A civil religion is not the 'religious life' as Oakeshott had identified it in 'Religion and the World'. There is abroad today, nonetheless, a call for a 'return to community' or for a new public philosophy to instil purpose and thus to overcome the 'politics of greed' and the decline into mere interest-group politics.

These and other similar formulations play on the tendency – even after the demise of communism as the worst case of modern rationalist politics – to cling to moralism, rationalism and scientism as plausible means to rectify or perfect politics. The West has not failed to see the perils of the most virulent forms of modern rationalism, but in the meantime its self-analysis has been unperceptive about its own rationalisms.

To avoid the mis-steps of otherwise admirable writers like Morgenthau and Lippmann, Oakeshott meditated, in hitherto unpublished essays, upon the vocation of the philosopher of politics whose understanding is of the sort Oakeshott had consistently maintained from his earliest writings. These writings show a strong affinity for the Socratic style of philosophizing in convicting the world of tending always to avoid radical assessment of its political assumptions. Oakeshott affirms for himself the philosophical vocation to engage in such questioning.

To affirm the philosophical response to politics means to accept the task of seeking philosophical understanding of politics in place of the task of seeking success in politics. A philosophy of politics cannot, for Oakeshott, be a prescription for political action or a political programme. Philosophy cannot be 'applied' to politics; philosophy can only understand more fully what is initially judged to be the character of political engagement. Philosophical insight involves a journey from more partial to less partial, but never final, knowledge. It involves critical reflection that questions the unexamined assumptions of political actors. Any distinctive mode of human endeavour takes for granted some assumptions. The character of such assumptions has much to do with figuring out the way in which the activity in question defines the meaning of experience as a whole for its own purposes. A mode of understanding with its assumptions is an interpretation of the whole of experience from a particular point of view. This point of view animates an activity and gives it an apparent basis from which to launch itself. But the price of constructing a launching platform is to ignore or fend off features of experience which do not fit easily with, or may even contradict, the point of view of one's activity.

In politics, Oakeshott argues, everything is to be made use of. Thus, for example, politics is not for contemplation or sheer present enjoyment. Rather, it is 'the means by which the institutional expression of approval and disapproval is adjusted to the gradual shift of judgement, and the means by which the integrity of the methods of satisfaction is preserved'. And 'what we desire to impose is already hidden in what exists' (what later, in 'Political Education', Oakeshott famously called 'the pursuit of intimations').

Political philosophers must start from the observable political world but, in reflectively considering it, they are moved to reflect even further on what has already emerged through earlier observation and reflection. All human activity is reflective. But there are various sorts of reflection: One sort Oakeshott calls 'reflection in order to serve', whose end is 'policy'. A second sort is reflection to achieve a 'doctrine' or explanation that aims to rationalize or give a unifying account of political activity. This is not the pursuing of intimations within ongoing political life, but the attempt to give an external account of how the goings-on of politics can be seen to be coherently related. This reflection seeks intelligibility by means of simplification.

Beside these there is philosophical reflection which is 'radically subversive'. Thinking philosophically is not 'having a philosophy'. The latter is antithetical to the former. Since there is no point at which philosophical thinking can suspend its reflection, there are no assumptions which can go unexamined. Philosophy is the engagement of continuous re-examining and, therefore, has no platform of its own of which it is not at the same time resolutely critical. As a consequence, philosophy can offer no guidance to anyone.

Moreover, philosophy appears to withhold from itself the prospect of religious fulfilment discussed earlier in this essay. Guidance assumes the satisfactoriness of a platform of self-understanding. Philosophy insistently confronts us with the argument that all platforms are infirm and dissoluble, even if all undertakings demand them. Philosophy is distinguished from other engagements by its constant attentiveness to its uncertainty, hence always reminding us of our own. Its interest in politics does not alter this; philosophy can only have a philosophical interest in politics, observing politics as politics does not observe itself, yet without intending to transform politics into some other activity than the one that was to be understood.

Philosophy is aware of politics in the context of all that is not politics, and thus cannot allow itself to operate according to merely political assumptions. Philosophy cannot, then, be transposed into a different thing called 'political philosophy' that is taken as a form of political action or guidance. Those who think in these terms merely disguise from themselves the disjunction between philsophical understanding and political action. Political philosophy is, strictly speaking, only the discovery of what must be true about political activity regardless of the aims and aspirations of political actors: political philosophy is

> saying something concerned with political activity such that, if true, things will be as they are; not as they were when we first caught sight of them, but as they permanently are. And here, as elsewhere, we must embark upon the enterprise itself if we wish to come to a clear understanding of it; there is no way of determining the end until it is achieved.

Oakeshott is saying that philosophy wants an account that illuminates activities going on as they do; philosophy does not choose an activity either in order to transform it into something else, or to somehow complete it, or to seek success within the activity's terms.[14]

The essays collected here are among those in which, over a

---

[14] Compare F. H. Bradley, whom Oakeshott admired greatly, in 'My Station and Its Duties': 'there cannot be a moral philosophy which will tell us in particular what we are to do . . . it is not the business of philosophy to do so. All philosophy has to do is "to understand what is", and moral philosophy has to understand morals which exist, not to make them or give directions for making them. Such a notion is simply ludicrous. Philosophy in general has not to anticipate the discoveries of the particular sciences nor the evolution of history; the philosophy of religion has not to make a new religion or teach an old one, but simply to understand the religious consciousness; and aesthetic has not to produce works of fine art, but to theorize the beautiful which it finds; political philosophy has not to play tricks with the state, but to understand it. . . .' *Ethical Studies*, p. 128. Consider also the argument of Socrates in Plato's *Charmides*: knowledge of the knowledges is at the same time a kind of ignorance since the philosopher's knowledge of a practice is not a practising of the practices. Consider also Leo Strauss: 'The difference between the philosopher and the political man will then be a difference with respect to happiness. The philosopher's dominating passion is the desire for truth, i.e., for knowledge of the eternal order, or the eternal cause or causes of the whole. As he looks up in search of the eternal order, all human things and all human concerns reveal themselves to him in all clarity as paltry and ephemeral, and no one can find solid happiness in what he finds paltry and ephemeral. . . . The political man must reject this way altogether. . . . He could not devote himself to his work with all his heart or without reservation if he did not attach absolute importance to man and to human things.' *On Tyranny, Revised and Enlarged* (Cornell University Press, 1968), pp. 211–12. There are differences with Oakeshott, but Strauss's view of the philosopher's attitude is similar.

period of thirty years from 1925 to 1955, Oakeshott elaborated for himself, but also to some extent confined, the religious and theological implications of *Experience and Its Modes*, worked out his political theory as summarized in *Rationalism in Politics*, and gradually assembled his philosophical account of the ideal that European civilization had made concrete in history – civil association under the rule of law – of which ideal he gave his definitive expression in *On Human Conduct*.

I

RELIGION AND THE WORLD

1929

'Pure religion', writes St James, 'is to keep unspotted from the world'; and with that, it appears, he forfeits all claim to our attention. For, if there be one idea more than another, among those which we suppose to have governed the lives of those early Christians, that provokes no assent, however qualified, in our minds, surely it is this – that religion consists in abandoning the world for a cloistered, if virtuous, existence, to which the word 'life' can scarcely be attributed. Religion, if it be no more and no other than this, is a pursuit for which we can find no place in any life we should wish to live, nor any response from the world of ideals our civilization has made familiar to us. It is a race for which we are unwilling to enter. Yet this other-worldly ideal still gains convinced adherents; and, indeed, it would be difficult to find any description, either of religion or of Christianity, which does not, in some sense, set it over against the world, or any religious ideal which contains no suggestion of escape from

> the fretful stir
> Unprofitable, and the fever of the world.

Thus, it would appear that we, who have some affection for life, and find this so frequently disparaged world not without merit, are the prototype of irreligion. Doubtless there are some to whom such a conclusion will cause no distress; but others, less ready to take the world and let religion go, may think it worth while to consider the question, what *is* this 'world', of which we hear so much and are bidden think so little? For, should our interest lie with religion at all, we shall scarcely be

27

content with the dogma that it consists in an escape from the 'world', when we know no more of the 'world' than that it is what the religious man must escape. For me, at least, it is difficult to believe that, in the young man, a precocious piety, and moral prejudice in the old man, are the only signs or are certain signs of true religion. Yet these are commonly accounted the marks of an unworldly life. And, moreover, the very unanimity with which secularism has been singled out as the chief enemy of religion, suggests that 'the world' shelters more than a single meaning.

For the early Christians, the world they described as dark and evil was the present age, or existing order of things. They lived in the immediate expectation of the Second Coming, which they pictured to themselves (after the manner of their time) as a sudden catastrophe which should make an end of the world and usher in a New Age. The world, for them, the present age and its political and social organization, the customs of their civilization, not the pleasures only, but the necessities of life also – these belonged to so unstable an order that to keep oneself unencumbered by them was the least provision one might make against the Day of the Lord. Religion, to them, defined as keeping oneself unspotted from the world, was easily understood and naturally agreeable. It implied, not the quasi-philosophical dualism of material and spiritual interests, but the more simple, more Hebrew notion of a dualism of historical periods. The age to come was imagined in no modern fashion to be the product of the existing age, their relations were sequential and not consequential; and merely to escape the entanglements of the present age was to qualify oneself to enjoy that which was to follow. Some it is true, 'having loved this present world', slipped back and were swallowed up in its darkness, but for most the expectation of the End was vivid enough to prevent irresolution. And, indeed, the vividness of the belief was its chief danger; it is difficult for us to imagine the dull fear, the creeping premonition that all was not as it should be, when delay ensued and the End was not accomplished. St Paul was among the few men who seem to have faced this contingency before it had become generally felt, and much of his life was spent in an effort to reconcile the Christian expectation of the end of the world with the disenchanting fact of delay. And out of this effort spring the Gospels, Christian theology and a new doctrine of the world.

For this new conception, which dominated the Middle Ages,

the world which is inimical to religion is not a mere period of time; nor, for the most part, did Christians any longer hope for a sudden end. The year 1000 AD had its trepidations and anxieties; but, those past, Christendom settled down to the notion that the life of one who has escaped the contagion of the world consists in a comparative freedom from material interest and a complete abandonment of any save the most elementary pleasures. The disparity between this world and the other world was no longer a matter of mere time, it was a matter of place: the material world was contrasted with a so-called spiritual world. To be unspotted from the world meant to live, without pleasure, a life so divided between this world and the other world that it required the invention of a whole psychology to persuade men of its possibility. This world of interests and activities, they believed would be with them to the end, but they must live in it as aliens. To it belonged their body and its senses, their mind and its ideas, knowledge and truth, art and literature, politics, patriotism, pleasure and commerce: every-thing save that pale and shadowy abstraction which they valued more than all else – their soul.

> Oh, wearisome condition of humanity,
> Born under one law, to another bound.
> Vainly begot and yet forbidden vanity,
> Created sick, commanded to be sound.
> What meaneth nature by these diverse laws?

Now, the idea that such a world as this should produce in us no desire but a longing to escape from it, is one with which we have little sympathy. Secularism must mean attachment to some world other than this so desirable world of intellectual and physical interests, if it is to be the enemy of any religion we should be distressed to lose. It is true that the medieval dichotomy between the natural and the supernatural is still convincing to some, but I do not think it satisfies most of us, and its power to satisfy is certainly diminishing. But this does not imply that there is no world from which the religious man will desire to escape; and I think there is something in the primitive Christian idea of the world which gives us a hint of a more satisfying view of religion, and the kind of secularism inimical to it. The bare expectation of the sudden dissolution of all that we mean by civilization is not, perhaps, less out of harmony with the view of things we should like to live by, than is the mere desire to escape from certain activities connected with that civilization, but I think it hides an idea, at once profoundly religious, and not so out of touch with the modern spirit as to be unintelligible to us. The mere fact that the expected end of the age was not accomplished in the manner he imagined, though disconcerting enough to the primitive Christian, was less destructive of his real beliefs than we might suppose. For his confidence in the coming dissolution of the world was as much the expression of a certain scale of values as it was a crude expectation of an historical event. Fundamentally he believed that history and the natural world must be held subservient to him, his life and his purposes; and, that the years should pass and nothing happen, need not shatter the force of this belief for him whose imagination it excites.

Here, then, is suggested a new dichotomy. The world which religion rejects is no longer a world of things and interests, but a system of beliefs, a scale of values. And the other world, to which religion belongs, is not a restricted world of narrow interests, carved out of a wider secularism, but, like its opponent, a system of beliefs and a scale of values. To keep unspotted from the world means, not to have restricted the field of our experiences, but to have remained uninfluenced by a certain scale of values, to be free from a certain way of thinking. Nor must this freedom be arbitrary; it must be sought with eagerness and held with passion. Religion is not achieved until we live in its world because we know that its scale of values and its way of thinking satisfy us more than any other. The other world of religion is no fantastic supernatural world, from which some activities and interests have been excluded, it is a spiritual world, in which everything is valued, not as a contribution to some development or evolution, but as it is itself.

I suppose, when we have rejected the crude dualism of the medieval view, the distinction between the world and religion would seem to turn most naturally upon material and spiritual values. And our belief in money, comfort, pleasure and prosperity, and the peculiar value we set on these things, is taken to distinguish us as worldings; while a life spent in the service of an ideal is some evidence of religion. But such a view is, I think, scarcely less superficial than that it is designed to replace, for it, also, does but relieve one element in our experience at the cost of another. What really distinguishes the worldly man is, I think, his belief in the reality and permanence of the present order of things.

RELIGION AND THE WORLD

The worldly man, as I picture him, believes in the fundamental stability of the present order, or that it will merely
evolve into another. The earth we tread, the species to which
we belong, the history we make, the communities we serve,
the sciences or arts to which we contribute seem to him
permanent; permanent, at all events, when compared with
those unstable things we call our *selves*. This belief implies what
may be described as an external standard of value: things are
imagined to have some worth apart from their value in the life
of an individual; and consequently, what is prized is success,
meaning the achievement of some external result. At worst,
perhaps, this ends in a life directed towards the building of a
mere reputation; at best, in one the meaning of which is looked
for solely in the contribution it has made to some art or science
or one of the other continuous activities of human life. History
and tradition, consequently, acquire an exaggerated importance, and the legacy of the past is often appropriated mechanically, as one might inherit an incipient disease or a volume
in a foreign language. The future is the Moloch to which the
present is sacrificed, and the life which leaves behind it actual
accomplishments is valued more highly than that which strove
to be its own achievement. With this belief goes, also, the
notion that a career is the main aim of life; for a career is the
only evidence a man has of external accomplishment, if he
make no contribution to art, science or literature. The safe way
is pursued, prudence is made a virtue, and, for the sake of an
hypothetical old man, who may bear his name thirty years
hence, the young man hoards his energies and restrains his
activities.

These beliefs – and there are few of us who are not saturated
with them – are the world, the only world truly inimical to
religion. Nothing can be certainly free from its influence; it lays
its hand upon art and literature, not dividing them, as before,
into secular and religious, but forcing upon them its ideal
of attainment, of history and of tradition – and under its rule
they perish. Religion itself is interpreted to follow this ideal,
becoming a pious antiquarianism, whose devotees, like the
Bourbons, learn nothing and forget nothing. It was from
this dark world and its elusive values that the childish and
erroneous belief about the end of the age rescued the early
Christians, by turning their attention from an ideal of external
accomplishment, which circumstances made seem so futile, to
one which, however little they were conscious of it, found in
the actual living of it the whole value of life.

But were we to embrace some similar but more credible belief, an·analogue of that old superstition, we should find that our values, also, would suffer a corresponding change. In place of the world's external standard of value, we should adopt a more personal standard. The ideal of success and accomplishment would be rejected for one in which the achievement striven for was the realization of a self. The 'vulgar mass called "work"', 'things done' would cease to have value in their result, but only insofar as they could prove themselves of worth as elements in the present experience of the most permanent and stable thing in life – our selves. Ambition and the world's greed for visible results, in which each stage is a mere approach to the goal, would be superseded by a life which carried in each of its moments its whole meaning and value. For, after all, could any notion of life be more empty and futile than this idea that its value is measured by its contribution to something thought more permanent than itself – a race, a people, an art, a science or a profession?[1] This surely is to preach an illusive immortality, to make humanity a Sisyphus and its life the pointless trundling of a useless stone. For, as like as not, if we set value upon external achievement alone, death or disease will rob us of our harvest, and we shall have lived in vain.

> Und eh man nur den halben Weg erreicht,
> Muss wohl ein armer Teufel sterben.

complains Wagner in *Faust*. And this must always be true when the meaning of life is sought in external accomplishment,

---

[1] Here also, if anywhere, is the conflict between science and religion. For science, human life appears as a brief interlude in the history of an insignificant planet, and the importance of human thought and sensibility is proportionate to the space and time it occupies in the physical universe. 'The whole universe', remarks Professor Jeans, 'is about 1000 million times as big as the part of space which is visible in a telescope which reveals about 2 million nebulae. Let us now multiply 1000 million by 2 million and the product by 1000 million. The answer (2×10^{24}) gives some indication of the probable number of stars in the universe; the same number of grains of sand spread over England would make a layer hundreds of yards in depth. Let us reflect that our earth is one millionth part of one such grain of sand, and our mundane affairs, our troubles and achievements, begin to appear in their correct proportion to the universe as a whole.' *Eos: or the Wider Aspects of Cosmogony*, p. 21. But to religion the importance of human life is always its felt value, which no 'scientific' argument can dictate or destroy. And that such a value would be considered 'unreal' beside the 'real' value of science is more than a little arbitrary. This 'universe' of physics is, after all, the creation of a particular and abstract kind of thinking on the part of an insignificant number of the insignificant inhabitants of this insignificant planet; and the relative *importance* of things is a subject about which science is powerless to enlighten us.

in extent of knowledge, in a career or in a man's contribution to art or science. But once we see clearly that the richest possessions are valueless apart from our possession of them by insight, the world's way has no longer any charm for us. The worth of a life is measured, then, by its sensibility, not by its external achievement of the reputation behind which it may have been able to hide its lack of actual insight. The legacy of the past will no longer be appropriated mechanically, for, when all opinion that is not the outcome of a living sensibility – no matter what the opinion be – is known to be merely parasitic and worthless, men see more clearly how dangerous it is to be an inheritor.

> *Was du erebt von deinen Vatern hast,*
> *Erwirb es, um es zu besitzen.*
> *Was man nicht nutzt, ist eine schwere Last,*
> *Nur was der Augenblick erschafft, das kann er nutzen.*

The religious man will inherit nothing he cannot possess by actual insight. He knows too well that 'it is but a windy happiness that is sought in titles taken upon others' credit' to desire to live upon the past, his own or that of others. Nor will the future be allowed, any longer, to lay its withering hand upon the present, for, though to live in the present may appear frivolous, to live for the future is certainly vain. And in knowledge, in place of an ideal of steady acquisition for some ulterior end in which, perhaps, he can never share, he will follow one which values it solely by its worth to present insight. And he will maintain a kind of candid detachment in the face of the very highest actual achievement.

The revolution required to establish this view of life would, of course, be immense, for in most respects it runs directly counter to our accepted opinions. It is regarded now as an ideal fit only for poets and women: this world is certainly 'too much with us' for its influence to be avoided easily. But, though we have no such belief as the expectation of the imminent end of the world to bring about this change, we have, I think, in the natural beliefs of youth, undimmed by the sordid demands of age and experience, a motive and foundation strong enough to produce and sustain it. In youth, before we have consented to take life as it is, before prudence has taught us the unwisdom of living ahead of ourselves, before we have succumbed to the middle-class passion for safety, regularity and possession, we believe that the most important thing is to preserve, at all costs, our integrity of character, for we believe that men, and not the things they create, are permanent and lasting. The length of art does not dismay us, for we are not conscious of the briefness of life. Indeed, this discrepancy between the length of art and that of life is altogether false, depending, as it does, upon the world's notion that art is to be found in galleries and libraries or anywhere except in a personal sensibility. In youth, this ideal is natural and agreeable; but the world is strong, and the savour of the ideal fades away as the disposition to flag grows upon us; for it is so much easier to imagine ourselves achieving our end by a career or a contribution, just as it is easier to know all about a picture than to achieve a sensibility for it. And this call of the other world – which can have failed to charm, at one time or another, but few – is gone like a cuckoo's cry, one moment near and the next far away. But, like that cry, sometimes it returns, though the intervals in which we hear it clearly are ever more infrequent as the world battens upon us. And I do not think it is merely a fancy to imagine a return each year with the Spring of this belief in the fleetingness of the things men do and make and the permanence and value of sensibility and possession by insight, and the consequent contempt for the world and its 'careerist' ideal. At all events, I do not know why we should be callous to the call of the seasons, and foolishly behave as if Spring and Winter were the same. In Autumn we mourn the Spring; in Spring we dread the coming Autumn; yet every Winter we forget how perfect the Spring may be. But, it is only those deaf to its language who do not feel a recurring inspiration to overcome the world, and those, though they may have gained the whole world, have lost their selves and with them all that has value.

Religion, then, is not, as some would persuade us, an interest attached to life, a subsidiary activity; nor is it a power which governs life from the outside with a, no doubt divine, but certainly incomprehensible, sanction for its authority. It is simply life itself, life dominated by the belief that its value is in the present, not merely in the past or the future, that if we lose ourselves we lose all. 'Very few men, properly speaking, live at present,' writes Swift, 'but are providing to live another time.' Such seems to me an irreligious life, the life of the world. The man of the world is careless of nothing save himself and his life; but to the religious man, life is too short and uncertain to be hoarded, too valuable to be spent at the pleasure of others, of the past or of the future, too precious to be thrown away on something he is not convinced is his highest good. In this sense, then, we are all, at moments, religious; and that these moments are not more frequent is due to nothing but our uncertain grasp on life itself, our comparative ignorance of the kind of life which satisfies, not one part of our nature, but the whole, the kind of life for which no retrospective regrets can ever be entertained.

A religious revival is sometimes preached and spoken of as if it could be quite independent of other conditions and without relation to anything save, perhaps, a stricter moral behaviour. But, since the religious life, in the view I have tried to represent it, is synonymous with life itself at its fullest, there can by no revival of religion which is not a revival of a more daring and more sensitive way of living. And such a life may as easily be stifled under a mountain of moral prejudice, as dissipated by moral experiment – perhaps more easily. Yet, if the reader is on the look-out for a more strictly moral application of what I have been saying I would by no means discourage him; on the contrary, beg him to consider whether it is not, after all, only an elucidation of what we mean by candour, and whether the religious or unworldly character might, not unintelligibly, be described as one the chief virtue of which is its sincerity. But, at all events, I think there is some evidence for believing that in this sense, the coming generation has the possibility of being more religious than its more settled predecessor. 'The youth of to-day', says a writer of some insight,[2]

> seems to me intensely interested in life; but, if I observe them rightly, it is life more as a means to experience, than as an opportunity for achievement, which absorbs and excites them . . . That life can be above all an opportunity for carrying out a preconceived plan, for striving towards a distant goal; that it should be crowned at last by that enduring fame which is the final reward of a rounded career, – this is an antiquated ideal.

We no longer ask for final wisdom, but for the freedom of the life unspotted from the world. The goal of life is not, for us, distant, it is always here and now in the achievement of a personal sensibility. And cowardice, the vice most antipathetic to religion as I see it – a willingness to prevent the influx of the

[2] L. P. Smith, *The Prospects of Literature.*

New, and resist its consequences – has for us fewer charms than it used. Conscience has made cowards of some generations, history and tradition of others, but a generation which would be religious must be courageous enough to achieve a life that is really contemporary. And then, in our age, as in all great ages, we might find more men living their lives and fewer merely hoping for life in some vague, ill-imagined future.

Perhaps it is because we, who are so much cumbered with the world's ideas, find it difficult to visualize this unworldly character, that we are so frequently driven to qualify it by negatives. To the world, religion naturally appears as a form of indifferentism or quietism, but it is not to be expected that the world should be in possession of the final truth in this matter. And, indeed, so soon as we begin to press these negative qualifications to their conclusion, a character grows before us, which, if it have no place in the affections of the world, at least is not wholly unintelligible to it. This, then, is the character of the religious man today, as I conceive him.

Unlike the typical medieval saint, he makes no attempt to leave the beauties and attractions of the visible world unseen, to subdue the flesh and curb the mind; unlike the primitive Christian, he is moved by no fantastic expectations; unlike the children of this age he is fascinated by no hope of a Good Time Coming. The world's ideal is achievement, it asks for accomplishment, and regards each life as a mere contribution to some far-off result. The past reaches up to the future, and the present, and all sense and feeling for the present is lost. From all these the religious man seeks nothing but escape; they are forms of the secularism which is the death of religion. He will keep in age youth's refusal to take life as it is, and the present condition of society will always cause him discontent. What governs him is not the world's ideal of visible achievement; life, for him, will mean more than a career, and he will not measure his success by the place he fills in some hypothetical development of evolution. The world and its 'careerist' ideal presents a whole miscellany of possible purposes for life, but all these the religious man will view as no more than distractions from its real business.

> The world
> Is full of voices, man is call'd and hurl'd
> By each:

36

but the religious man, undazzled by these glories and un-imposed on by these values, seeks freedom, 'freedom from all embarrassment alike of regret for the past and calculation on the future', freedom from the encumbrance of extraneous motives and parasitic opinions, which is the sole condition of the intellectual integrity he values more than anything else. Life to him is not a game of skill, people and events are not counters valued for something to be gained, or achieved, beyond them. In the extemporary life he deserves to live, nothing is of final worth except present insight, a grasp of the thing itself, and the only failure to fall back on that 'anodyne of muddledom' by which men seek to substitute mere extent of knowledge, or a career, or this idea of a contribution, for the too difficult task of attaining a personal sensibility.

Memento vivere is the sole precept of religion; and the religious man knows how easy it is to forget to live. But he has the courage to know what belongs to his life, and, with it, steps outside the tedious round of imitation by which the world covers up its ignorance of what it is alive for. He loves life too much to pay too highly for mere existence – to pay with his self. He is not among those who are ready to live at any price; the condition upon which he has engaged to live is that he will take nothing in exchange for himself. He has a horror of vileness, not of death; and to make a living without making something of life is vile. Life, for him, is well lost in an adventurous cause, for that is one way, at least, of winning it. And the only immortality which fascinates him is a present immortality; 'so far as is possible he lives as an immortal'. The world has an immortality which it preaches, an immortality found in some far distant, future perfection of the race, but it practises death. For, in the world's view, human life is an insignificant episode, brief as a dream, it is only the hoarded achievements of men which are real and substantial; and it requires every man to pay away himself. But what shall a man take in exchange for himself? *Wenn wir uns selbst fehlen, fehlt uns doch alles.*

The religious man, though he may take himself seriously, will not bore others by letting them know that he does so, because it is only in the world's view that a man in better off for being known to be what he is; for religion it is enough to be it. And, that the world should wreak its vengeance upon those who deny its view is only to be expected, but the world's vengeance harms none but the children of the world. And those who have cultivated a contempt for the world have discovered the means of banishing it.

This, then, is the religious man, who sees all things in the light of his own mind, and desires to possess nothing save by present insight. For him the voices of the world have not drowned the voice of youth and life. Firm in the possession of himself, he lacks nothing. Fear has no meaning, safety no charm, anxiety no occasion, and success is bound up with no dim and problematical future. He is unspotted from the world:

> From the contagion of the world's slow stain
> He is secure.

2

RELIGION AND THE MORAL LIFE[1]

1927

There is a view that religion stands outside what we ordinarily think of as the moral world. To be an initiate is to be transferred entirely from the moral world of rights and duties into another world; for the moral world and all in it is evil, a veil between us and God. But to most of us this will appear both abstract and extravagant. To us it seems obvious that there must be some connection between religion and the moral life – if only we could discover it. And, indeed, it is easy enough to discover it in a practical way. 'A man who is "religious" and does not act morally, is an impostor, or his religion is a false one.' But here we have chosen a less easy task – to try and see the connection between religion and the moral life not merely practically, but theoretically and as a whole.

This connection has been conceived of in various ways; but, in the main, they reduce themselves to three.

> Religion as morality itself.
> Religion as the sanction of morality.
> Religion as the completion of morality.

Let me describe them in this order:

1. In its crudest form the notion that religion is morality is both familiar and absurd, though perhaps not so familiar nowadays as it was when expounded by Comte, his disciples in positivism, and the 'ethical societies' of the end of the

---

[1] A paper read at a meeting of the D Society on 19 October 1927.

last century.[2] All that need be said is that religion as wholly identified with morality is a travesty of human experience expressed by means of an abuse of language. Nor will it greatly help us if we say that 'Religion is morality touched by sentiment'; for in the end this turns out to mean that it is morality touched by *religious* sentiment, and we have gone no nearer the truth.

But there is a modified form of this view which is of extreme importance, and we may characterize it as 'Morality as the condition of religious belief'. In its simplest form it is just honesty with oneself. 'Rather would I not finding, find Thee; than finding, not find Thee,' says St Augustine; and in the same way Renan speaks of himself as 'forsaking Christ for Christ's sake'. And it is only a more complex and refined form of the same idea which is the fundamental notion of Dr Oman's *Grace and Personality*.[3] Relevant to our point, the main thesis of the book is this. Religion if it is an activity of human beings must be the activity of moral personalities; and no religious doctrine or notion can properly be called 'religious' if it does not accord with the requirements of moral personality. 'We constantly look at life religiously and morally, as through a binocular out of focus. At best we dimly feel these worlds are one; . . . at worst we shut one eye and look morally, and then shut the other and look religiously.' This separation Dr Oman finds reflected in Christian theology, with disastrous effect; especially in the traditional doctrines of Grace. In these, the question which is taken to require an answer is, how would God seek to display his majesty, his dignity, his omnipotence? Whereas the true question is, what, amid all he does for us, is the end he seeks? And the true answer is that the end he seeks is to succour moral persons. Since religion is a relation between God and moral persons, all notions of irresistible grace operating mechanically are impossible; for the characteristic of moral personality is its autonomy. 'An order imposed by God otherwise than through our own sense of right . . . would be no true moral order. Nothing is morally observed which is done as

---

[2] A more recent presentation of this view is to be found in A. Loisy, *La Religion*.

[3] John Wood Oman, philosopher and theologian, was born in 1860 and died in 1939. Educated at Edinburgh, he was Professor of Systematic Theology and Apologetics at Westminster College, Cambridge, 1907–35, Moderator of the General Assembly of the Presbyterian Church of England, 1931, FBA 1938. His principal works were *Vision and Authority* (1902), *Grace and Personality* (1917), and *The Natural and the Supernatural* (1931). (*Timothy Fuller*)

the exaction of God's will. It must, even if it be only in submission, be the expression of our own.' 'Action, though otherwise not wrong, is less than right, unless we, of our own insight, judge it to be right.' 'Blessed art thou if thou *knowest* what thou doest; if not, thou art accursed and a breaker of the law.' And these conditions of the truly moral life are the conditions also of religious beliefs. And thus, our relations to God and His to us are not religious in one aspect and moral in another, but moral because they are religious and religious because they are moral.

2. Our second view, characterized as 'Religion as the sanction for morality', has often been taken as specifically Christian, though hardly through any intrinsic merit or reasonableness, and to dispute it has sometimes been regarded as synonymous with questioning the validity of Christianity. The argument is as follows.[4] Naturalism as a basis for moral law fails; a basis for morality cannot be found in the natural individual as such, it must be sought in some 'higher sanction'. And Christianity, it is said, holds that morality must be something revealed to us as an expression of God's will. There is nothing particularly complex in this position; its whole emphasis is, not only upon the incompleteness of a morality based on so-called 'nature', but upon the fact that there is no alternative save a morality founded upon a revealed religion and drawing all its sanction, as a morality, from that foundation. But this view has various implications, some of which I shall notice later.

3. Our third view I have called 'Religion as the completion of morality'. This view is perhaps best summed up in the words of Pascal: '*Il est bon d'être lassé et fatigué par l'inutile recherche du vrai bien, afin de tendre les bras au Libérateur*' (*Pensées*, 422). And it has both Bradley and Bosanquet for exponents. Morality is self-contradictory and so, to a degree, abstract. There are two aspects of this self-contradiction of mere morality, one implied in the other. In the first place, it says to the individual 'You *ought*, you *ought* to be equal to the situation,' and says no more. The good is imperative on you here and now, and you are to bring it about by your own effort. But out of every moral success the further 'ought' springs up to condemn you once more: it is a series without an end. And in the second place, morality as it is built up and preserved in the

---

[4] An argument of this character distinguishes Mr Thornton's book, *Conduct and the Supernatural*.

moral sense of a community is something changing, growing, purifying itself, but with no hope of a final end where it can rest. The good is never finally achieved either individually or socially; morality tells us to realize that which can never be realized; the moral life is a 'vain search after the true good'. 'We have at furthest the belief in an ideal which in its pure completeness is never real; which, as an ideal, is a mere "should be".' But this is not enough for religion, though for mere morality it is amply sufficient; abstractions can live, and live only in an abstract world. In the religious consciousness there is the belief in an object other than myself; an object, moreover, which is real. What in morality was a mere 'should be' in religion becomes an 'is'. The good is discovered to be real and to be achieved. In religion we achieve goodness, not by becoming better, but by losing ourselves in God. For goodness is never achieved by becoming better: that is the self-contradiction of morality. Religion, then, is the completion of morality, not in the sense of a final end to an historical series, but as the concrete whole is the completion of all the abstractions analysis may discover in it. Religion is not the sanction of morality, but the whole of which morality is an aspect, and in which mere morality perishes, that is, is discovered as an abstraction.

Now, the degree in which these notions conflict depends upon the view each implies of the nature of religion and the nature of morality. We must, then, ask ourselves what views of religion and morality lie behind the notions of 'Religion as the sanction of morality', 'Morality as the condition of religious belief', and 'Religion as the completion of morality'; and how far do they exclude one another. And I may be allowed to change the order of treatment from that of genesis to that of adequacy.

1. In 'Religion as the sanction of morality', since morality fails to find a basis for itself, religion must step in and show morality as something wholly objective, as coming down upon us with an authority not its own, as something revealed to us as the will of God; and this is sometimes claimed as the achievement of Christianity. The moral law, then, is something foreign to 'natural man', it is something which God reveals to him and commands him to obey; and for Christians this is revealed in the Gospel. Morality consists in obeying God's commands; religion is the revelation of morality as the command of God. This is a simple and apparently Christian view

of things, but I believe it to be both immoral and unChristian. And its best refutation is to be found in an examination of the meaning of religion and morality contained in the view of 'Morality as the condition of religion' as expounded by Dr Oman.

2. For Dr Oman moral personality and moral action mean absolute independence. 'Moral responsibility requires absolute, not partial independence.' The distinguishing characteristic of moral persons is autonomy: to a moral personality nothing is of value except through personal insight, we can keep the law only by *knowing* what we do, not simply by obeying blindly. Religion, on the other hand, requires absolute dependence on God. Nothing less will suffice; it is impossible to divide the allegiance, to depend partly on our own moral freedom and partly on God. Complete self-surrender is necessary in religion. But this absolute moral independence and absolute religious dependence are not opposites but necessarily one and indivisible; 'for we serve God only as we are true to our own souls, and we are true to our own souls only as we serve God'.

Here, then, is a refutation of 'Religion as the sanction of morality', over and above the formal contradiction implied in the two views. If the moral law is the command of God which has merely to be obeyed blindly, then we are moral immorally – which is absurd. If morality consists in the autonomous moral personality choosing and understanding for itself, then the notion of an external moral law, the will of God, is an immoral notion. And if a religion reveals the moral law as something which requires mere obedience, then that religion is false. It was a tenet of 'Religion as the sanction of morality' that the basis of the Christian code of morals is contained in the sayings of Jesus as recorded in the Gospels. But these, according to Dr Oman's argument, are valueless *per se*, for they do not become moral until they are accepted by an autonomous moral personality. By themselves they are devoid of moral significance. Just as the truth 'revealed' in Christ must be seen as having its evidence in itself before it is properly understood, so 'nothing is moral which is done as the mere exaction of God's will'.

And yet, though 'Religion as the sanction of morality' is, I believe, destroyed by 'Morality as the condition of religious belief', this leaves us still unsatisfied. And our dissatisfaction comes largely from what I believe to be its inadequate account of the nature of morality, an account which is supplemented, but not substantially contradicted, by that of 'Religion as the completion of morality'.

3. The distinguishing characteristic of moral personality upon which Dr Oman lays his emphasis is its autonomy; but is this all that we mean by morality? Is moral action nothing more than this 'conscientious action'? or do we need to add a certain kind of knowledge to autonomy before we achieve concrete morality? It seems to me that autonomy is merely the *form* of moral personality and action, which requires some definite content to rescue it from abstraction. Free action is not moral action unless it is also wise; and it is just this element of wisdom which requires definition.[5] For, after all, although we admit that knowledge of anything is not true knowledge unless it is personal insight, acquired and mastered by an individual mind, we recognize that there is something other in knowledge than this 'autonomy', and we have other standards of truth and falsehood than those of mere personal insight. And just as knowledge consists in something more than the individuality of its acquisition, so moral action comprises something more than the mere autonomy of the actor. A concrete moral action is the autonomous, free, *and adequate* reaction of a personality to a situation. And this is where 'Religion as the completion of morality' has a more adequate view of moral life than that proposed by 'Morality as the condition of religious belief'. And if we say that morality is knowledge, a certain kind of knowledge, we do not thereby deny the necessary autonomy of moral personality; rather, we assert it, because autonomy is the form of all knowledge worth the name.

Here then, I believe we have a more adequate view of the relation of religion and the moral life. Morality is this endless search for the perfect good; an endless, practical endeavour resulting in momentary personal failures and achievements and in a gradual change of moral ideas and ideals, a change which is perhaps more than mere change, a progress towards a finer sensibility for social life and a deeper knowledge of its necessities. But, nevertheless, a battle with no hope of victory, a battle, in fact, in which a final victory is the only irretrievable defeat. And what is it that urges us on to these moral in-

[5] Readers of Dr Oman will recognize that I have done him less than justice. Though his emphasis goes the other way, he too recognizes that autonomy is only the form of moral personality, a form which both governs and is to be filled out by the whole content of Christianity – a position, nevertheless, not without its difficulties.

novations, that gives insight, energy, and power to invent and to refine in the moral life, where achievement is convention, and convention only a seed which, except it be cast into the ground, cannot live? What is it that, without attempting to supply a sanction, shows the whole from which this endless 'ought to be' is an abstraction? This, I think, is what we call religion; the motive power, the growing point and the completed whole of merely moral ideals.

Religion as nothing whatever to do with morality is an abstraction; religion as morality is a travesty of human experience; religion as the mechanical 'sanction' of morality is a superstition; morality as the limiting condition of religious belief is true but does not go far enough or tell us all we want to know; Religion as the completion, or 'ideality', of mere morality seems to me the least inadequate of the theories which human insight has suggested.

But let me end on a practical note. How shall we best think of the relation of Christianity to our moral life today? Christianity has produced a whole view of life, a definite civilization; our moral ideas are to a large extent inspired by what we understand the Christian view of life to be, and changes in our moral life may be brought about as we understand our religion more fully and experience it more simply. Religion, it is true, has effects other than this of producing a new moral outlook, it is primarily the view of the whole, the inspiration and the energy which makes us personally continue this 'vain search after the true good'; but in doing this it produces also our changing morality. The only morality Christianity has yet produced is our morality, for a morality cannot exist in a book or a vague ideal or anywhere except in an active sensibility. Christian morality is not the whole of Christianity, is, in fact, a mere abstraction so far as religion is concerned, but it grows with the deeper understanding of Christianity; and, for these reasons, and without permanently identifying Christian morality with any one particular phase of civilization (as it is sometimes identified with the Apostolic age or the Middle Ages), I am unable to recognize the gulf which many writers allege to be fixed between what we call civilization and Christian morality.[6]

---

[6] Those acquainted with his writings, will recognize how much I am indebted to F. H. Bradley throughout this discussion.

3

SOME REMARKS ON THE NATURE AND MEANING OF SOCIALITY

1925

We know that we have passed out of death into life through love of the brethren.

John, I. iii. 14

Only insofar as men live after the guidance of Reason do they always necessarily agree in nature.

Spinoza, *Ethica*, IV. Prop. 35

The essence of Reason being, indeed, nothing but our mind in so far as it understands clearly and distinctly.

Ibid., IV. Prop. 26

A society may be looked at from two sides, we may see it made up of individual selves, and we may see it as making, being the substance of, those selves. The one view is not more an abstraction than the other; the whole is like a medal which, though we can ordinarily see but one side at a time, is essentially made up of both sides. It is of no great moment how we name the essence of this social whole, and if we choose to say that 'sociality' is the central principle of its being, we have still to ask ourselves, what is sociality? However, having given a name to the thing we are out to capture, we must now in the words of Plato be 'like hunters surrounding a cover and must give close attention that the thing itself may nowhere escape us and disappear from our view: for it is manifest that it is somewhere here; so look for it and strive to gain a sight of it'.[1]

---

[1] Plato, *Republic*, 432 B. 'Sociality' must be understood if the 'political life' or the 'good life' are to be understood. The latter are terms of uncertain meaning despite their common usage.

THE NATURE AND MEANING OF SOCIALITY

In general, those thinkers who have failed to win any clear vision of the nature and meaning of this thing which we have called the law of the life of a society, have made either or both of two mistakes. Sometimes they have entirely mistaken the kind of thing for which they were looking, and while it was actually in their hands or 'rolling before their feet' they have taken no notice or even cast it back into the sea; and at other times they have gone about to capture their prize with the most ludicrous equipment imaginable, thinking it a prime necessity to take council with the savages of distant parts of the earth (instead of the wise men of the past and of our own day). For, in their estimation, one custom gathered from the life of the poorest savage, nay, even from the life of the animals themselves, has more weight than the most considered pronouncement of the wisest of men. As a result of the first of these misconceptions, sociality has been confused with mere sociableness (in the vulgarest sense of the word). This, indeed, no more than follows the popular notion that a man is rightly branded unsociable who, no doubt to his misfortune, is not blessed with a natural grace of manner and readiness of behaviour, and that he, above all, is sociable who possesses the discretion and *usage du monde* which is called politeness; but popular error is a sorry justification for philosophical dimsightedness. And again, it has resulted in the idea which is behind the contrast of society and solitude, the notion that the proper opposite to the social man is the recluse. St Bernard with his '*O solitudo, sola beatitudo*' and Hegel with his (tacit) '*O societas, sola felicitas*', are deemed to have contradicted one another;[2] but such is not the case. And yet again, it has led us to the use of false and misleading metaphors when we have tried to set forth the nature of a society. We have thought to describe the *vis vitae* of a society in terms of mechanics as if it could rightly be compared with a machine or a problem in statistics (and our talk has been full of such phrases as 'centre of gravity', 'equilibrium', and the 'resolution of forces'). Or, we have turned to biology and imagined that society may be described as an organism. It has even been maintained before the Utilitarian society that revolutions in social organizations are explained and justified on the grounds that they are comparable to biologic mutations. But for such attempts there is no warrant, and they can only be explained by the extraordinary

[2] See George S. Santayana, *Soliloquies in England*, p. 119.

infatuation to which our minds have been subject ever since the great biological discoveries of the last century began to be popularized and misunderstood. Of all the fanatic, explain-all principles which have dimmed our vision this one of biology is perhaps the most signal exemplar of our capacity for prejudice in matters of the mind; and if its strength has now begun to fail, modern psychology has stepped into its place with all the signature of an authentic panacea.

The other misconception under which we have laboured with regard to the central principle of the life of a society, is that which has mistaken the means by which it may be discovered; and this brought with it other and not less alarming consequences. Its most striking bequest is the firmly entrenched confusion between the gregarious instincts and true sociality. Instead of saying with Aristotle, ἡ φύσις τέλος ἐστιν, we have persuaded ourselves that the most primitive, we sometimes call it, the original, manifestation of a thing not merely shows the real nature of the thing, but *is* its real nature.[3] As it happens, it is those who know least about these primitive conditions who have always shown themselves most eager to uphold them as the only criteria for judging present circumstances. However, while this form of argument was used with engaging simplicity and colossal ignorance by the Voltaires of the eighteenth century, it made for itself a firmer foundation in the nineteenth century by entering upon an immense study of primitive conditions and original forms, but as yet it has failed to prove, or even attempt to prove, that in so doing it has actually carried us nearer to the discovery of the real and whole nature of things. It has been said that it is not the sociality of man's nature which distinguishes him, for 'there are many animals which not only have a social life, but a social life much more complex and perfect than that of men'.[4] And Francis Galton tells us:

> It has been my fortune, in earlier life, to gain an intimate knowledge of certain classes of gregarious animals. The urgent need of the camel for the close companionship of his fellows was a never exhausted topic of curious admiration to me during tedious days of travel across many North African deserts. I also happened to

[3] The damage which this notion has done to the understanding of religion, and especially Christianity, is, of course, quite beyond exaggeration. It has distorted our whole outlook on the subject, and raised a kind of atavistic ideal which itself is a throw-back of mind of no mean order.

[4] Windelband, *An Introduction to Philosophy* (1921), p. 254.

hear and read a great deal about the still more marked gregarious instincts of the llama; but the *social animal* into whose psychology I am conscious of having penetrated most thoroughly is the ox of the wild parts of western South Africa.[5]

But all this talk of 'social animals', and all these examples of ants and prairie-dogs, only serve to demonstrate the utterly erroneous view of the true nature of sociality in human life which prevails in so many quarters. That ants may appear to us to have an organized life of a very definite character is no more than the truth, but on these grounds, to call their life 'social' in the same sense as human life is social has no shred of justification. And the cause of the misconception lies in the fact that we have been content to see the essence of sociality in some kind of governmental organization or instinctive attraction which is common to men and many species of animals. But to suppose this, is to suppose that there is the same mental condition and history of the mind behind the laugh of the prowling hyena and the laugh born in the essence of great comedy. Even when we have left behind us this consideration of the habits of animals as explanatory of the habits of men, we are not permitted to relinquish the logical fallacy which led to its inception. We are told that 'the original and elementary subjective fact in society is the consciousness of kind', and that this 'acts on conduct in many ways, and all the conduct which can properly be called social is determined by it'.[6] It may be true that we can best understand this primitive instinct of consciousness of kind as the ignorant, blind, experimental expression of true 'sociality', just as we may regard the human sacrifices of antiquity and primitive races as the ignorant expression of a true belief that 'life is not the highest good', that there are things and values to the glory of which mere living is a pale shadow, but this is the reverse of saying that the primitive instinct guides and rules the more developed faculty for society. The truth is that no talk of herd-instinct or consciousness of kind even begins to touch the true basis of a society (or to enlighten its *vis vitae*). It is all entirely beside the point. And even when we advance sufficiently in our studies to say that 'neither in savagery nor in civilization do men normally live in isolation',[7] and to quote William James as saying

---

[5] Galton, *Inquiries into Human Faculty*, p. 48 (italics mine).
[6] Giddings, *Principles of Sociology*, p. 19.
[7] Giddings, *Ibid.*, p. 81.

that 'to be alone is one of the greatest evils for normal men',[8] we do not even make an entrance upon the true subject of our study. Sociality has nothing whatever to do with men's instinctive desire to escape from isolation, nor can it be defined in any terms of non-isolation or physical impulsion. These are not grounds upon which we may properly pronounce either animals or men to be social beings.

The process of our argument up to the present has been somewhat as follows. The essence of a society, its law of life, which we have for our own convenience called sociality does not submit to purely naturalistic explanation. We must seek elsewhere for a true vision of the whole fact of a society. If we may make a distinction which cannot be finally upheld, society is a moral fact and not a natural fact; it is a feature of the life of minds in relation, not bodies in proximity. Consequent upon this comes the necessity of discovering something more about this moral or 'good life' if we are to see clearly what sociality is. The attempts which we have reviewed have all failed to enlighten us because, either they fail to see that what we are trying to get at, and what we must try to get at if we are to see clearly the nature of sociality, is a coherent conception of the 'good life', or they misconceive the manner in which it is possible to reach this conception. Now, besides mistakes of this kind there are others into which we may fall of a less ridiculous nature but which nevertheless preclude our seeing sociality as it really is. A theory of society may be wrong because it is not a theory at all, or else because it is wrong even though it sets about the task in what we conceive to be the right manner. Of this latter sort there are not a few examples in the history of philosophy and it would be asking too much to demand that they should be passed in review before any attempt is made upon the problem on our own account. But there is one theory which, by reason of its plausibility and popularity, demands that some notice should be taken of it. And in remarking upon it I wish to take it as an example of the kind of inadequacy from which a theory may suffer.

Bentham and Mill worked out in their Utilitarianism an idea of the 'good life' and, very properly, demonstrated the way in which it appeared to explain the facts of human society. They saw clearly enough that short of such an idea, all that we could say about society and sociality was so much wasted

[8] McDougall, *An Introduction to Social Psychology*, p. 85.

breath as far as philosophy is concerned. But this did not ensure that their theory embraced all the facts of human life. The most interesting feature of the formulation of the Utilitarian philosophy which we owe to Bentham, is that it immediately set in motion a train of speculation which in the end was forced to deny many of its original propositions. From Bentham, with his purely hedonistic account of moral action, to Mill, who begins to recognize the real difficulty in applying this idea to the actual societies in which men live, there is a great development. Bentham never attempted to answer the question, why is the general happiness desirable to the man whose only good is personal happiness? Mill made some attempt to answer it,[9] but in so doing exposed an even more fatal inadequacy in the theory itself. But the development did not cease with him. The particular defects which he exposed have been taken up and answered by Sidgwick, who in turn has shown an even deeper inconsistency in the theory. But while what may be called the hedonistic element in this philosophy has developed, another of its features has remained constant, and it is with this which I am concerned. 'By Utilitarianism', says Sidgwick, 'is here meant the ethical theory that the conduct which, under any given circumstances, is objectively right, is that which will produce the greatest amount of happiness on the whole; that is, taking into account all those whose happiness is affected by the conduct.'[10] This constant characteristic of Utilitarianism, as exhibited in this passage, and which is to be found, for instance, in a much earlier pronouncement of this same philosophy, Butler's 'Sermon on Forgiveness', is the manner in which it divides the life of the individual and the life of society into exclusive areas and so destroys all idea of a whole except as a kind of average condition of being. The individual self can never be quite certain when he is promoting the good of the 'whole' that he will not be forced to exclude himself from that good, and on the other hand, it is always possible that in seeking his own good he may be denying the greatest good to the 'whole'. Now, in place of the 'whole' in this theory, it is clear that we must write the 'rest' – and this is the vital point. To the Utilitarian there can be no social whole – for a 'whole' which is divided into 'self' and 'others' is no whole at all. 'It is the right of the State', says

---

[9] J. S. Mill, *Utilitarianism* (1863), p. 53.
[10] Sidgwick, *The Methods of Ethics*, p. 411.

Fichte, 'to employ for its purposes *the whole surplus* of all the powers of its citizens without exception.'[11] And here again appear the ideas of a 'surplus', of exclusive areas of obligation, and of a divided moral sanction. So far as its theory of sociality is concerned this is the key to the Utilitarian position, and it is clear that it is hardly short of a denial of the possibility of sociality in any true sense. The possibility of sociality, that is, the possibility of a society, rests upon the discovery that in the end moral obligation cannot be divided into exclusive areas, but is a single and self-sufficing whole. It rests upon a unity which is not merely a practical unity of action created out of a kind of average, lowest common multiple, but a unity of mind based on, and arising from a real wholeness and comprehensiveness of life. By this time it will become obvious that the particular disability under which this theory labours is a misconception of the nature of society and of the self, which has naturally led to a mistaken manner of relating them. Here then is the vital question for us to decide. We can have no clear view of the nature of society until we have penetrated the secrets of the self. This is just what the Utilitarian philosophy fails to do.

On the subject of the self I can offer here no more than a few scattered observations. (Of the self I have already said something.) It is not a psychological analysis (that is the analysis of one abstracted aspect) that we now require, but some deeper insight into its whole and real nature. But in this matter it is not psychology, but law, which has led us astray. We shall never discover the secret of the self or of anything else, if we are not prepared to go beyond the conceptions which are necessary for practical conduct. Difficult as are the situations raised by the interplay of finite personalities in the affairs of life (and no one has penetrated that difficulty more seeingly than Hebbel in his dramas, *Judith* and *Giges und sein Ring*), the problems which a view of the self as such, and for its own sake, raise, are still more baffling. Time and again the relation of the finite self to the universe has shown itself to be the hardest problem with which modern philosophy is faced, and it does not loom so large in the writings of the earlier Utilitarians only because they were not properly aware of its full implications. And short of a view of the place which the finite self must take in the cosmos, we shall not begin to have

[11] Fichte quoted in Sorley, *The Theory of the State* (ed. Bryce).

a true view of its relation to other selves; the one relation gives meaning to the other. 'Now do you conceive it possible', asks Socrates, 'to comprehend satisfactorily the nature of the soul without comprehending the nature of the universe?' And Phaedrus can but answer, 'No'. In the world, the experiences which begin to unlock to us the nature of the self are parting, separation, bereavement and, most penetrating of all, exile. To travel among a foreign people and to be ignorant of their language is to experience an acute diminution of the content and expressiveness of self; to live among them ignorant of their customs and divorced from their manner of life, is to become acquainted with the real content of self; to dwell permanently in exile from all that is nearest to us, country and countryside and friends, is beyond doubt the greatest tragedy our life affords. Not because these things give us the elementary experience of physical separation – though that is true enough – but because they lead us to see past that, and recognize the isolation of mind which is their essential nature. And it is the realization of this that admits such cure as the case allows. For Solon or for Dante it is not primarily the separation of body which counts, and for this reason they are the greatest of all exiles.[12]

In thinking of the self, the mistake which we are most prone to make is that of confusing the bodily appearance, the physical unit, with the true self. What strikes us most in viewing selves as bodies is their isolation, and the application of this notion to the real self has issued in such errors as the confusion of sociality with mere sociableness, and the superficial contrast between society and solitude. So far from it being permissible to identify sociality and sociableness, we may not even take the latter as evidence of the presence of the former, even in its most elementary appearance. Nay, it is probable – and such indeed is what the experience of life leads us to conjecture – that the man who is not in the vulgar sense sociable, has in him the more intense experience of the meaning of society and sociality. For such a man needs and looks for an intense unity with those with whom he associates; acquaintanceship to him means nothing, and each new entrance into the social experience calls forth all his affection and desire for a perfect oneness of mind. To him the shell, the mere form of sociableness, without that which can give it a vital meaning, is the most painful experi-

[12] 'De Vulgi Eloquentia', i. 6.

ence he can undergo. It is often the most retiring who are in the real sense most sociable, for short of this intense union, which is society at its greatest, they are not content with, or at ease in, mere cohabitation. (It is this feeling which confronts us again and again in Wordsworth's poetry, and which is at the heart of the poetic experience of A. E. Housman.) We must look elsewhere for the root of sociality than in this its poorest and meanest expression. Those who have known only sociableness have not entered a society in any true sense.

Our mistaken notion that society may properly be defined as the opposite to solitude arises from the same confusion of the self with the body. There is a sense in which, as Epictetus says, 'solitude is a certain condition of a helpless man' when he has been bereft or something of somebody on which he had depended to the extent that it had become a part of himself, and this, indeed, might be taken as the true meaning. But it is not with this that society is ordinarily contrasted. It is supposed that the self is discovered in solitariness because it is then most clearly seen to be distinguished from the environmental not-self. But such a notion is untenable. The solitude which men desire is that which reveals to them a more harmonious self than that which they can find in the physical presence of their kind. The solitude which they desire is that which is society. The recluse is thought of as essentially a man who has retired from the social whole in which life is ordinarily passed, but this is not so. The essence of his life is that it is passed in the closest communion with those people and things in which he can find his self most fully. He does not draw apart in order to break his connections with the world, but in order to find them, and make them stronger and more vital – for they are the self. It may be with books, it often is with the great figures of history and of poetry that such a man finds his life. And this life of imagination is a thousand times more social than the common life of the majority of people who pass their time in closest physical proximity with their kind, but who never experience the real essence of a life in society. It is the social spirit itself which may impose this merely physical apartness on a man. The solitude which he finds is what Charles Lamb calls a 'sympathetic solitude', for he understands that 'solitude sometimes is best society'. This is true also of the man who goes to be 'alone with nature', unless it be in answer to some mawkish world-sickness and fancied superiority to other men that he leaves their presence. This type of mind is seen, perhaps, at its greatest in Wordsworth, who finds satisfaction in 'nature' simply because of his deep imaginative sense of the unity of things and his experience of the inexpressiveness of the vulgar distinction between 'man' and 'nature'. He seeks, not solitude, but society. *Nunquam minus solus quam cum solus*. Like Byron, he had experienced that

> There is society, where none intrudes,
> By the deep Sea.

It is not an experience which comes to everyone. Dr Johnson preferred Fleet Street to an evening walk in a deserted Greenwich Park, and it is not, perhaps, the highest experience of society; but we do not see it aright unless we see it as society and not as some empty, negative solitude. (Nettleship, in a letter written from Corfu, makes an interesting and true comparison between the society of nature and the society of men.

> I suppose love of solitude and reverie are almost confined to Teutonic people. I can't make out whether one is higher or lower for having it. Sometimes it seems as if it *could* only be a second-best thing to have communion with nature: and I do believe that, if the same sort of feelings which are now set going in me sometimes by simple natural life could be continuously set going by every human being I came across, I should be a much higher animal than I am. Nature does not stir desire, and the interest in nature seems perfectly disinterested. But if one could get right through the desire and the fear which clog one's intercourse with one's fellow-creatures it would be a diviner air still that one would emerge into.[13])

It was Spinoza who said: 'Except man, we know of no particular thing in nature in whose mind we can rejoice. With nothing else can we unite in friendship, or any kind of social life.'[14] And friendship to Spinoza was life's highest prize.[15] Solitude is desired and is desirable when it reveals the self, when it affords that society which may become most intimately a part of the self. The physical presence of our kind, and the delights which it brings with it, are desirable only when these, also, enter the self and become part of it. Not until we break

[13] Nettleship, *Remains*, I. 74.
[14] *Ethica*, Part IV, Appendix S26.
[15] *Epistolae*, XXII (Bruder's edition, II. 222).

down this barrier, the contrast between society and solitude, shall we begin to see what is the true nature of sociality. We must seek elsewhere than in this vague and well-nigh meaningless contrast for the law of the life of society.

On similar ground is the assertion that we must find the basis of society in some gregarious or herd-instinct, only here it is not a wrong conception of the self which bars the way, but a total lack of any conception at all. It is true that a gregarious instinct of some sort is the basis of society in exactly the same sense that it is true that pen and ink are the basis of Dante's *Divina Comedia*. The poem could not have been written without some such instruments, just as society could not exist without some sort of physical basis; but it is a great delusion to suppose that for this reason these instruments and this physical basis help us in any way to explain the whole and real thing. Gregariousness has not more to do with community, than mere association has to do with logical unity, the things are of a wholly different nature. An example will illustrate this. The gregarious instinct leads men and animals to congregate together. It is an instinct which has an obvious utility in times of danger and an equally obvious utility as creative of conditions of greater ease and comfort of life. Under its guidance the effort to find food came for the first time to have some semblance of organization, meals were no longer solitary (they probably never were), but were partaken of in company. But it has long been recognized that a change from such a state of affairs as this, to life in a real society necessitated some sort of revolution. To explain this, men (according to the customs of the time) cast their explanation in an historical form and pictured to themselves some conventional agreement which should mark it. Or, like Burke, they were forced to imagine that somehow or other a change came about in the 'nature' of man, for clearly his nature in society is different from that which he possessed before society came. Since then, we have abandoned this semi-historical form of explanation, but still have before us the facts to be explained. The form we use is logical, and yet there still clings to it a suggestion of history, of one thing following another in time, though this is in no way part of its real meaning. As we enter society we enter a *vita nuova*, or, in the expressive words of St John, we 'pass from death to life'. The meal which was instituted for the sake of life and whose institution was presided over by the gregarious instinct and all the other instincts, exists for the 'good life' or the excellence of souls. In society, a meal is no longer merely a means of satisfying hunger, we do not eat in order to be filled; it is an expression, full of meaning, of true sociality. The trivial objects which grace the board have a poetic religious and moral significance which, present indeed at every meal, is found at its highest when religion, as it so often has done, makes them the centre of the intensest social unity. It is not mere chance or historical accident which has led men to make a meal the central act of religious communion, it is an expression of the meaning which society puts into things when it comes to dominate the order of our life. The difference between the gregarious instinct and true sociality is that which lies between the beast's hasty and oft interrupted satisfaction of hunger, and the 'love-feast' of a religious community.

The delusions which we have suffered by our infatuation with mechanical and biological metaphors for explaining the nature of society have resulted in a permanent blindness to the difference which exists between the things which make it necessary for men to live together and depend on one another, and those which form the true basis of a social whole. Men live together by reason of many of the necessities of life, economic necessities, necessities of physical strength and necessities of instinct, but none of these has anything to do with society as such; nor are we able to explain the ultimate tie between men as consisting in personal interest or personal pleasure. This is what the English Utilitarians attempted, but they did not succeed. To assure ourselves against many of the delusions of the past the first precaution we should take is not to speak of society in any other terms or metaphors than those which actually concur with the nature of the thing itself. Society is not a machine or an organism, it is a spiritual whole, a unity of mind. Metaphors from mechanics do not explain it, nor does biological life. That which has been held to explain it, that which (*me judice*) does explain it more and more perfectly as we come to understand it better, has been called by many names. Plato called it justice, Aristotle says friendship, of modern writers (most of whom have not found it necessary to depart from these old names) Balfour calls it loyalty,[16] but the best name, because the most comprehensive, is the principle of the good (that to which Christianity has given the name – love). But even here we are not free from the confusion into which

---

[16] Balfour, *Theism and Humanism*, p. 106; Royce, *The Philosophy of Loyalty*.

the misuse of words is continually leading us. Love and friendship are often identified with their lowest and least comprehensive manifestations, even with things which bear only a
superficial *similarity* to them, and their nature is mistaken.
Scientific writers speak of the sexual instinct as love, and so
attribute it to animals.[17] And we are all familiar with the
grotesque use of the word '*amour*' which disfigures the novels of
Anatole France. Nevertheless only in this thing called friendship, so often in the minds of Plato and Aristotle, only in this
thing called love, recognized by Paul as the only explanation of
the nature of a true community, can we find the essence of
sociality, the meaning of society. And let us not at this point be
dragged from our path by the illogical suggestion that the
societies of our experience rarely show this characteristic. We
have answered that argument before, and answer it again – it
is no argument at all, any more than an objection that it was
not black would be an argument against calling a diamond,
carbon. A life in society means a unified life; the essence of
sociality is to give unity. Not the unity of mere association, but
a logical unity. And to give life a logical unity is to give it what
it else had not – a meaning. 'Do you not know', says Epictetus,
'that as a foot alone is no longer a foot, so you alone, are no
longer a man?' And why? Not because of the interdependence
of modern economic conditions, not because of the division
of labour, but because, if we understand ourselves, we see
that 'aloneness' and 'self' are contradictory. Life viewed as a
whole and for its own sake, knows no such thing as aloneness.
Biological life may give us the illusion of separateness, but even
if it gives us the opposite impression, that of the unity of the
species, it adds nothing to the concept of unity which is now
before us. Human life is not to be fully explained by biology:
biological man is an abstraction, though a useful one. It was a
principle of Roman law that the man who was alone was no
man at all, but this again adds nothing to our argument, for
man's life is not to be fully explained in the terms and conceptions of law. Legal man is an abstraction, though a very
useful one. The unity of which I speak is the unity of life and of
mind which we call love and friendship. Without that unity
society could not exist. It is a necessary postulate for the facts
of human life when they are seen in their wholeness.

[17] 'A dog is continually scratching himself, and a bird pluming itself, whenever
they are not occupied with food, hunting, fighting, or love.' Galton, *Inquiries into
Human Faculty*, p. 18.

THE NATURE AND MEANING OF SOCIALITY

The real life of a society is expressed most clearly in terms of love/friendship, of the principle of the good, and to venture upon the discovery of the true nature of these is at once the final and the most difficult chapter in our account of the self and its life. To pause for a moment and see how far we now are from the speculations on governmental form and organization which occupy the major part of our political 'philosophers' today, is to see how far modern political philosophy has strayed from a true view of its proper subject matter.

It was a wise dictum of Aristotle that the perfect law-giver has more regard for friendship than for justice, for the latter cannot exist except in a society founded upon and moved by the former. We cannot see law and government as they really are except as an effort, of a particular and limited nature, to further the ends of a society of this nature.

But, to return to our subject. It will not surprise the attentive reader of the history of political philosophy, that the thing which has been universally singled out as giving as deepest insight into the nature of love and friendship, themselves the essence of sociality, is religion. It is a large and difficult subject which I have neither time nor ability enough to treat as adequately as I should wish and as it demands. It were, perhaps, better not to treat it at all than to approach it hastily, but since it is the very essence of the position I am putting forward, some hint of its meaning must be given. Briefly, the position is that God is the only principle of sociability which will explain the facts of life. Society becomes possible by religion. When I say that no society has existed or can exist without religion I am not making an anthropological assertion as the deists of the eighteenth century vainly strove to prove in the dawn of the historical method. I am giving it as part of my definition of a society, a definition which seeks to view the principle of its possibility and the law of its life. Recall Plutarch saying that a state might more easily exist without a geographical site than without belief in the gods. Plato reiterated the same thing and Socrates suffered in his effort to bring his fellow citizens to a better view of religion. Aristotle saw in religion the only foundation to the life of the state.[18] Rousseau, by the preconceptions of his age about the nature of religion, was driven to express his sense of the need of it by postulating

[18] *Politics*, VII. 8. 7.

the necessity for a *'religion civile'*,[19] and in our own day Bernard Bosanquet has reached the same conclusion.[20] Two of the writers who have treated this subject most comprehensively have received but scant recognition for their services to the theory of society, but in what I have to say now I shall in the main follow them. The first is St Paul, and the second, in many respects following him, is Spinoza. All unity in human minds depends upon a devotion to the highest ends which we know; unity exists only in so far as such a devotion is present. Men are united, society is society, only in so far as they live after the guidance of reason. The good is the child of reason, and so, in the words of Keats writing to one of his friends, 'the higher the degree of good, the higher is the degree of Love and Friendship'.[21] And God is the life of reason. It may seem a poor descent from poetry to prose to translate the great discovery that 'God is Love' into 'God is the only principle of sociality', but I think it lets us into the secret of its real meaning, and the real extent of the discovery. Just as to Plato it was clear that the measure or depth of the unity of a band of pirates is in exact proportion to their justice, so to us it appears that the depth of our sociality is proportionate to this devotion to the highest good we know, which we call religion. Love and friendship are the essence of sociality, and the life of these is hid in religion. To say more, without venturing upon a complete treatment of the theory of society and the state were both undesirable and impossible.[22]

I can see no better conclusion to this matter than a word on a subject much in our minds during these years, but of which force of circumstances has conspired to obscure its real nature. I mean patriotism. If a society be what I have contended that it is, and if patriotism may be taken as a complete devotion to the ends of our society, our state, then to me patriotism is the motive which should guide us in all our actions. And not only this, but that it is the motive which does rule in our minds

---

[19] *Du Contrat Social*, IV. 8.

[20] *Philosophical Theory of the State*, p. 309. *The Social and International Ideals*, p. 16. *The Principle of Individuality and Value*, Lecture X, Appendix XII.

[21] *Letters (Colvin's edition)*, p. 188.

[22] I may refer to Spinoza, *Ethica*, Parts IV and V, *Tractus Theologico-Politicus*, chapters IV and XVI, and *Tractus Politicus*, chapter II; also to Duff, *Spinoza's Ethical and Political Philosophy*, chapters X and XI. Perhaps I have not made it clear enough that I take Love and Friendship as the essence of sociality only because the principle in which they live is 'the good'. Finally, I should always come back to the good as the only principle of sociality.

insofar as we are truly members of our state. The reality of our membership is in proportion to the intensity with which we recognize and live by this motive. In this sense (and it is the sense which alone can be admitted as true on the principles of truth and definition to which I have adhered) patriotism is the basis of all morality, in short, is the greatest emotion and intellectual effort of which we are capable. It is a poet's patriotism perhaps, but for that nonetheless true. It is not that which is stigmatized as 'the last refuge of a scoundrel', it has nothing whatever in common with the pomp and pride and vanity of those who boast of what they neither understand nor feel aright. But it has many expressions short of that which is of the whole, and unalloyed. We cannot refuse to acknowledge something real in the impulsive love of country and country-side which plays so great a part in the life of most of us. The feeling that, as Coleridge says,

> There lives no thought of feeling in my soul
> Unborrowed from my country! O divine
> And Beauteous island!

leaves few of us unvisited, but in most it does not rise beyond an isolated sensation. But above and beyond this there is that strong intellectual love of our state, unmarred by false and partial views of the nature of love and the thing beloved, which we must count as the highest expression of the highest that we know. This is the whole and real thing which gives meaning to those blundering expressions and pitiful mistakes into which men have fallen in this matter.

> Some for a gentle dream will die:
> Some for an empire's majesty:
> Some for a loftier humankind,
> Some to be free as cloud or wind,
> Will leave their valley, climb their slope.
> Whate'er the deed, whate'er the hope,
> Through all the varied battle cries
> A Shepherd with a single voice
> Still draws us nigh the Gates of God
> That lead unto the heavenly fold.

Poetry it is, but good philosophy too –

> And life, some think, is worthy of the Muse.

I have been betrayed, at the end, into the expression of a view of things which the preceding arguments have but imperfectly justified. And yet, if they have been followed with attention, there can be little danger of the tenor of my suggestions being misunderstood. In these remarks I have done little more than throw out a series of suggestions and hints, first in criticism of the views of society and its meaning which are widely held today and which I believe to be entirely false, and secondly in an attempt to build up what I think a better and more comprehensive view. These suggestions are to a certain extent disconnected, or, at any rate, ill-connected; but there lies behind them a fairly consistent theory of the character of social life to which I am unable at present to give as connected an account as I would wish. They, like the finite selves in the philosophy of Plotinus, all move round a single conception, but do not always fix their gaze upon it. They are like a choir of singers standing round the conductor, who do not always sing in time because their attention is diverted from him. But when they look at him they sing well. So, these hints are consistent inasfar as they truly agree with the notion of society I have at the back of my mind and they partially express my meaning, but often I am conscious that they depart from that consistency and become isolated and feeble parts of a whole which does not exist.

4

THE IMPORTANCE
OF THE HISTORICAL
ELEMENT IN CHRISTIANITY

1928

Since what I am able to offer you can in no sense be called authoritative, may I explain at the beginning that what I propose is simply to present a point of view – a personal point of view insofar as it is mine, but something, I hope, a little more valuable than merely personal in that I shall try to set out, as clearly as I can, the reasons which lie behind it. The difficulties of the subject are great enough to demand a more tentative attitude than that which I have adopted, but if I speak positively rather than meticulously, I do so to avoid ambiguity and not to affect dogmatism.

That the historical element in Christianity has been regarded of the utmost importance to our religion cannot and need not be denied. On the contrary, so far as we can see, with the growth of Christianity the importance of this element has increased rather than diminished; indeed, the sensitiveness to what is 'historical' in Christianity appears to have reached something of a climax at the present time. And this circumstance raises, for me at least, two questions for which reasonable answers of some kind should be found. They are

1. What is the historical element of Christianity which has been regarded important? and

2. Does the fact that it has been held to be important mean that it is necessarily and permanently as important as it has been held to be?

An answer to the first of these questions has been provided for us already. The historical element which has been regarded important in Christianity is not the obvious fact that Christianity is a 'founded' religion, not the fact that Christianity (in a sense) did start at a given date (for that is equally true of a great number of religions which in a more significant sense have little use for history in their beliefs); nor is it a simple recognition of the value of tradition in religion; but, rather, what it has been held to mean is a belief in the *necessity* of that which is *prima facie* historical, or the historical as such. Christianity, so this interpretation runs, by the assertion of the necessity of certain events having taken place, put forward a view of the time-process which gave it a significance and a value which it otherwise could not possess. The atonement is a unique and necessary historical event. I need not enlarge upon this view, for it is one with which we have all been familiar since childhood; it is the traditional interpretation of the meaning of the historical element of Christianity.

The second question, however, permits no such simple explanation, and the fact that it has usually been answered in the affirmative must not deter us from examining the grounds of such, or any, reply. The assertion that this element of Christianity is necessarily as important as it has been held to be, implies, and has usually been consciously associated with, one of two theories of the nature or identity of Christianity. Christianity has been identified either with the whole original Christianity, which is held to include this particular belief; or, with a central core, of which this particular belief is a part, which has remained unchanged throughout the history of our religion. These two theories of the identity of Christianity are not always distinguished with the care required to see them clearly, and since both have been taken as grounds for an affirmative answer to our question, I must do my best to explain them a little more fully.

The first argument is this: Christianity is the whole original Christianity; this includes a belief in the necessity of the *prima facie* historical; therefore this belief is essential to Christianity. The minor premiss is an historical statement which I do not venture to question, but the major contains a theory of the identity of Christianity which is open to logical criticism. Christianity, it says, is the whole original Christianity; if something today proposes itself as Christianity and yet differs in any respect from the original thing, then it is not Christianity. The records we have of that beginning are the criteria by which alone we may judge the Christianity of an idea or doctrine or practice. 'To say that Christianity survives, even if weakened and disestablished, is to say that the Renaissance and the Reformation are still incomplete.'[1] This is not a new theory, nor one peculiar to Christian theology. 'In this consists identity,' says Locke, 'when the ideas [or things] it is attributed to vary not at all from what they were that moment wherein we consider their former existence, and to which we compare the present.'[2] It is the theory of identity without difference, the theory by which difference of any sort destroys identity; and its defects have frequently been pointed out. Its principle is simply that 'everything is equal to itself'; it says nothing more than that A is A, and that any change whatever in A causes it to become other than A. Indeed, we may not speak at all of a 'change in A'. It excludes from the thing all the differences of its states, attributes and relations, and the result is nothing more than a barren tautology. An arbitrary line is drawn across the change and variety of the process of history, and identity is denied merely at the point at which some little education is required to recognize it. How arbitrary that line is in the case of Christianity is at once apparent; for where is this absolute original which, unchanged, is the real thing? We have no knowledge of an unchanging, original Christianity which existed at one moment in time, absolute and whole, to change which is to produce something other than Christianity. The New Testament is a record of change and development; at what point did this development cease to be Christian? The 'teaching of Jesus', as we have it, is neither comprehensive nor thoroughly coherent, and a view of Christianity which identified it with the 'religion of Jesus' would exclude any beliefs which may have attached themselves to the experiences resulting from His death. Nor are we able to propose a selection from the beliefs and facts of those early years, for it is essential to the theory before us that *every* event and belief (up to a point which it is impossible to determine) is equally necessary to Christianity. This theory seems to me as unsatisfactory as any could well be; and it is unsatisfactory for the purpose of identifying Christianity because, and only because, it is unsatisfactory for identifying anything.

If, then, an affirmative answer to the question, is the historical element of Christianity necessarily as important as it has been regarded? were to depend upon such a theory as this,

[1] Santayana, *Winds of Doctrine*, p. 37.
[2] *Essay*, II, xxvii. 1.

we could be forced to declare it a groundless assertion. But we have before us another theory which has also been taken to support an affirmative answer to our question. Its argument is as allows: there has been a history attached to Christianity, there have been changes, but Christianity itself is an unchanging core or centre which has persisted through change; this particular belief in the necessity of the *prima facie* historical is part of that core; therefore it is an essential part of Christianity. Here again the minor premiss is an historical statement of which I need say nothing; it is with the major we are concerned. The theory of identity which this argument implies may be characterized as identity of substance. It is, perhaps, only a modification of the first theory, for it, also, demands an identity without difference. This core or centre which is Christianity has been variously conceived; it has been thought of as a general tendency moving through the history of our religion, as a spirit informing it, or as an ideal or purpose guiding it; but whatever it is, the only change it has been thought to suffer is that produced by the mere passage of time, though this itself implies a formal contradiction. In all its forms it is an excessively vague theory; it admits differences but leaves them as anachronisms; they are regarded as, at any rate, partial destructions of identity. But the chief objection to it is that it makes Christianity out to be a bare and bloodless abstraction, a wretched fraction of any of our experiences, such as we are convinced, when we are not defending a theory, it can never be. Though it is true that some parts change more slowly than others, it is only the barest abstraction that can show no change at all, something which occurs alongside the facts, the historical facts of Christianity, something we can deduce but never experience, surmise but never know. Those who believe in this theory, and they are not a few, may be invited to show us this unchanging central substance. We should imagine that it might be found by whittling away the differences and so exposing the thing, but when all the differences are gone we shall discover that what remains, so far from being our religion, is 'an invulnerable nothing'. Like pure water, it has no taste.

In various ways, then, what may not unjustly be called the current theories of the identity of Christianity break down, and until we can find a more tenable theory to put in their place we not only lack grounds for an affirmative answer to our question, but grounds for any answer.

THE HISTORICAL ELEMENT IN CHRISTIANITY

I cannot pretend to have a complete and unassailable theory of identity to offer you, and in place of such a theory I will venture the following by no means original suggestions. Identity, so far as Christianity is concerned, must be discovered in the facts of history, not as something unchanging, or some substance common to them all, but as a kind of qualitative sameness. Identity, so far from excluding differences, is meaningless in their absence, just as difference or change depend upon something whose identity is not destroyed by that change. It is not a matter of size or shape, or of anything so abstract as spirit or purpose; on the contrary, it seems to lie, first, in the avoidance of any absolute break in a thing's existence, and, beyond that and governing that, in some qualitative element to be discovered only by reference to the general character of the thing concerned. On this view of identity – and on no other, so far as I am aware – the characteristic of being Christian may properly be claimed by any doctrine, idea or practice which, no matter whence it came, has been or can be drawn into the general body of the Christian tradition without altogether disturbing its unity or breaking down its consistency. This means that an idea or practice may properly be Christian which, in part at least, runs counter to much that had previously been regarded as Christian. It means, also, that the identity of our religion is maintained, not in spite of, but because of, differences and changes. To apply the second and governing criterion of identity it would be necessary to come to some definite conclusion about the general character of Christianity, which is too large an undertaking for the present occasion. But the kind of way in which I should be inclined to think of it is like this. Christianity is a religion, and while it is not a characteristic of religion to remain unchanged throughout human history, it is one of its characteristics continually both to conform to and to lead what may be called the civilization or culture of its adherents. There is no religious idea with which we are acquainted which has remained entirely unchanged. To identify Christianity with its whole original state (if that could be found) or with some unchanging core (if that could be known) is to deny its nature. A religion must, somehow, represent to its believers the highest they can believe, the best they can desire. Such beliefs and desires do not remain unchanged, and so Christianity either is something which can maintain its identity and at the same time be the highest our or any age can believe or desire, or it fails to be a religion in the full sense. And, to me, the failure of Christianity to meet the demands put upon it by present requirements would be more certain evidence of its demise than almost any alleged break in the Christian tradition. In short, the argument is this: religion is characterized by its power to give life and to give it abundantly; Christianity is a religion; and therefore it can properly be said to maintain its identity while continually admitting perhaps wholly new ideas and practices, no matter whence they come, and while continually discarding perhaps thoroughly traditional ideas and practices, so long as the modifications are effected in such a way as to cause no absolute break in the development and to comply with its general nature as a religion.

The result of my argument so far is, then, that although the belief in the necessity of the *prima facie* historical has been regarded as an important element of Christianity, we cannot assert that it is *necessarily* either so important as it has been held to be, or even important at all, until we have tested it by a sound theory of the identity of Christianity; and according to the theory of identity I have suggested, whether or not this belief *is* important to Christianity depends upon circumstances. It is, then, only by considering these circumstances that we can hope to discover any grounds for delivering a rational judgement of the value of this belief.

The value of a specifically religious idea or belief is, in part at least, to be judged pragmatically. It might be possible (indeed, I do not think it would be difficult) to show that a belief in the necessity of the *prima facie* historical is a belief in something very much less than reality, something in itself inconsistent and therefore theoretically worthless, but such a demonstration in this place would be both frivolous and irrelevant. Religious ideas, unlike philosophical ideas, do not depend entirely for their value upon a demonstration of their ultimate truth: they have another purpose, the fulfilment of which is subject to a pragmatic test. To the philosopher, then, who should tell us that our faith in history is pathetically misplaced, we may answer that the question before us is not the ultimate reality of historical events, but whether or not a belief in the *prima facie* historical is a permanent religious need which demands some kind of satisfaction. Those apologists, I think, are in error who say that Christianity has ever, in any ultimate sense, asserted the essential reality and uniqueness of all events and of time, for such an assertion is no part of a specifically religious belief, and Christianity is first and last a religion. But Christianity certainly has asserted a very general need for some kind of religious belief in the necessity of the *prima facie* historical, and, if we may judge from the past history and the present state of our religion, this assertion is very well grounded in fact. There has been, and there seems now to be, a very general need in the religious consciousness of Christendom for this kind of belief in history. But before we use this as an argument to establish that belief as an important and even necessary part of Christianity we should, I think, consider the following facts.

This belief and need for belief in the necessity of the *prima facie* historical, besides having some foundation in human nature in general, was inherited by Christianity, like so much else, from Judaism: it is what has been called 'the Jewish principle of considering as the object of religious emotion a something which has occurred once for all'. That, of course, is not to say that it cannot be in the fullest sense Christian, but I think it should make us more critical of it than we might otherwise be, for '*gefährlich ist es, Erbe zu sein*'. By some means or other, perhaps through the instrumentality of Christianity itself, this belief in history has, since the eighteenth century, become part of our normal *Weltanschauung*; this peculiarly Hebrew belief, which had little or no counterpart in Greek culture, has been westernized. I need hardly offer a proof of this. The tremendous power of persuasion exercised by an historical analysis over uneducated minds was magnified in the nineteenth century to immense proportions. All intellectual effort had a tendency to run to history, and the reading of history became itself a means of grace and even a religion.[3] The consequence of this is that a certain artificial and inflated demand for history and a belief in history has been created. We *believe* in history; it is part of our religion because it is part of our mentality. But this ideal of *wie es eigentlich gewesen* is little better than an illusion, and its apotheosis, *passéism*, is a sign of the times: history and not conscience, in these days, does make cowards of us all. But, as far as our civilization is concerned, so much belief in history seems to be working its own ruin; the intellectual energy of our generation is turning in other directions, and the power to stand on the point of the present is returning. This artificial and inflated demand for a belief in

---

[3] Troeltsch, *Der Historismus u. seine Probleme*. Schweitzer, Civilization and Ethics.

history is, then, not necessary, but the creature of a period, and when it disappears, as it seems like to do, its counterpart in Christianity will be seriously lacking in any real contact with the normal outlook of our civilization. We should, I think, also bear in mind that the necessity for this belief has often been denied by many religious men brought up in the Christian tradition. We cannot assert that it is a need universally felt even among Christians.

Our conclusion, then, if I may venture to state it definitely, is that this belief in the necessity of the *prima facie* historical shows no sign of permanence or necessity. It has a long and honourable history in Christian tradition; it has undoubtedly been held an essential part of Christianity; but I can find no adequate reason for supposing that it is so. Lacking it, Christianity, it seems to me, would not lose its identity, were the modification to be effected at the demand of a religious consciousness educated in our religion. Our second question must, then, be answered in the negative.

It is a comparatively simple matter to detect inadequacy in ideas and systems of ideas, but we can claim to have performed no useful service until we have pointed to the affirmative ground upon which our negatives are based. And the state of affairs I have detailed, like all negatives, demands its positive complement, which I can best supply, as I see it, by asking two more questions.

1. Is the belief in the necessity of the *prima facie* historical the only interpretation of the historical element of Christianity?

2. And, if not, what other interpretation is there which gives us greater insight into this element of our religion?

I have tried to make clear that what we have been examining is only the traditional interpretation of the historical element of Christianity, and the rest of my argument would, I think, go to support a suggestion that there might be another view of the matter, no less Christian and a little more logical. The traditional view is a crude interpretation, the work of naïve religious minds seeking a theory of any sort rather than of critical minds seeking consistency. It is without philosophical plausibility, or, when we see it clearly, any lasting practical value, for what practical value it possesses depends upon a condition of mind neither permanent nor essentially Christian. But I believe that there is another and better interpretation of this felt necessity for the historical and of the particular satisfaction Christianity has afforded it.

THE HISTORICAL ELEMENT IN CHRISTIANITY

Religion and the religious consciousness, as I understand them, are essentially practical. A religion, in a manner to which a philosophy is not subject, may be proved lacking by being proved inadequate to the demands of the ordinary life of ordinary people. Our felt wants are, of necessity, the starting point of our religion; not the complex desires of that kind of sophistication which would see clearly the nature and meaning of the universe as a whole, but the simple needs inseparable from an active and practical life. Religion exists to satisfy no craving for knowledge apart from the knowledge which comes with the mere strength and courage to take life as it is and 'turn its necessities to glorious gain'. One of these felt wants, one to which the religious consciousness is particularly sensitive, is the need for an almost sensible perception of the reality of the object of belief. Religion demands not that the necessity for the existence of what it believes in should be proved, for that is an academic interest, but to be made intensely aware of the actual existence of the object of belief. A kleptomaniac may know that it is wrong to steal, but he does not know it in such a way as to feel it. And a philosophic proof, for example, of the necessity of human immortality has little or no religious value. We cannot love or live upon the knowledge of a mere necessity; love and life demand an immediate awareness, if not of the senses, at least of memory and mind. The thoughts of religion must also be feelings in that they must possess the force and liveliness, which we connect with feeling, to strike the mind and compel not merely acquiescence but action. Religions have replied to this demand in various ways; and no religion has left it entirely unanswered. Some have depended upon ritual to create this living contact between the believer and the believed, some upon the actual presence of that which is worshipped, some upon a visible representation of him. Idolatry is an expression of this need, a crude and primitive expression perhaps, but, so far as we can see, a necessary stage in the development of this element of religion.

One of the revolutions which Christianity proposed to the religious consciousness was that this actuality, given the necessary preparation of mind, could be more fully achieved on a higher plane; it proposed a religion more purely spiritual, yet one which should give an intensity of awareness of the object of belief so far denied to those who clung too closely to sensible actuality. Like other religions, it developed its rituals and its sacraments; but, unlike many others, by the emphasis it placed upon history, upon the actual happenings of the life of its founder, it removed from sense to memory and mind some at least of its power to give actuality to the thing believed. The historical element of Christianity took the place of cruder and more primitive methods of providing this necessary actuality. 'A Christianity without sacraments', it has been said, 'could never have converted Europe,' and perhaps its greatest sacrament was what we call its historical element. 'When historical examples are pointed out to us, there is a kind of appeal, with which we are flattered, made to our senses, as well as to our understanding,' says Bolingbroke in his *Letters on History*, and how potent the historical is to satisfy this craving for immediate awareness, every generation of Christians testifies.

What has the paraphernalia of historical evidences to do with spiritual need – not the temporary and immediate need which is satisfied only by immediate consolation and confidence, but the more permanent need of the religious consciousness of finding an intellectual world in which to be at home? To this question, then, our answer has been that in the crude and obvious sense history and the historical have little or no connection with spiritual need – are, indeed, something almost foreign to it – but in a more subtle sense the connection may be real enough. It has been argued that the demand of the religious consciousness for an individual and unique experience is itself a demand for a belief in the necessity of the *prima facie* historical, but it is, I think, a false argument. What religion demands is not a consciousness of the necessity and individuality of past events, but a consciousness of the individuality of present experience. What Rickert calls the 'principle of uniqueness' is something which is, indeed, to be found in history, but is to be found also, and found independently, in the determination of present practical life to face 'the irrepressible New' and achieve some measure of freedom from the past. And because religion is nothing if not contemporary, the historical element of our religion must be interpreted so as to give it a permanent and not a merely temporary meaning. In place of the old interpretation of the historical element in Christianity, that it means simply and crudely a belief in the necessity of the *prima facie* historical and is merely a denial of the Christ-myth, I would put this other interpretation, that this element of our religion means that the necessary actuality of the object of religious belief must be sought continually on a higher plane than one of mere sense, and that when sought there it will be found more intensely than ever before. And the path which it points us to ends in the achievement of a sensibility for which such a belief in history also is an idolatry.

The conclusion, then, at which I arrive is that the historical element of our religion is not necessarily historical at all; that is, its essential characteristic lies not in a belief in the necessity of the *prima facie* historical, but in its provision of the required actuality for the object of religious belief. Ritual and sacrament minister to this same need, and in some respects labour under fewer and less serious theoretical deficiencies; and, while this belief in history is justified by its fruits, it is justified only so long as it bears those fruits. What I have tried to show is that the ability of the historical element of Christianity to achieve its end, that is, to give actuality to the believed, depends upon a certain mental outlook neither peculiarly Christian nor necessarily permanent. It is not to be doubted that we shall always possess a certain susceptibility to history and its power to give life to thought; what varies and what is by no means permanent is the degree of that susceptibility. The Jews possessed it in a very high degree, and the culture of nineteenth-century Europe was vividly conscious of it, but our generation seems to share that sensitiveness less and less intensely, with the consequence, not that Christianity is dying, but that the presentation of it must in this respect change to changing needs, becoming, and not for the first time, a religion in which no servile archaeology inhibits vitality or chills imagination. On some of the current theories of the identity of Christianity such a change would imply a destruction of our religion, but I have tried to show that it is these theories which are fallacious and not our religion which is moribund. What that change will amount to in detail I must be excused from predicting, but that we can change much without ceasing to be Christians is the view I have suggested and for which I have endeavoured to find a logical apology.

THE AUTHORITY OF THE STATE

1929

It may appear tedious merely to press one or two elementary
questions back to their fundamental constituents, and it will
certainly be called academic. Yet I think, on the whole, it will
save our time, for the resolution of all the important problems
in this or any subject depends upon the answers we find for a
few elementary questions, and to consider these first enables us
to do once what it might otherwise be necessary to repeat a
hundred times, and then to less purpose. For example, there is
no question concerning authority, its power or *locus*, which we
can so much as discuss rationally until we have achieved some
coherent notion of what authority itself is. Consequently, and
because I have none but elementary ideas on the authority of
the state to offer, I propose in this paper to consider three
questions. First, what do we mean by authority? secondly,
what do we mean by the state; and thirdly, where, then, is the
authority of the state?

What do we mean by authority? It seems to me that, at first
sight, there are three ways of answering this question. It may
be suggested that it is unnecessary to go beyond what is
commonly understood by the word: or if, as we shall discover,
the common meaning be not entirely unambiguous, all we
require is agreement upon some definite meaning. 'When we
do not know the truth,' says Pascal, 'it is well that there should
be a common error to fix the minds of men.' Should we,
however, wish to discover the truth, we shall, I think, find
ourselves obliged to adopt neither of these, but a third course.
The common meaning, as such, will satisfy us no more than a
merely agreed meaning; what we desire is a coherent and
unambiguous conception of authority. We must, no doubt,

start with the common meaning of the word, but we can escape its inconsistencies, not by agreeing upon some arbitrary definition, but by transforming them into a coherent whole. And that is what I propose to attempt.

There are two points in the common view of the meaning of authority which appear to me ambiguous. Authority is conceived, in the first place, as both external and coercive. It is external in the sense that it takes the place of first-hand experience, and where such experience exists, authority is superseded and disappears; and it is coercive, not because there can be no kind of appeal from it, but merely because it does not itself attempt to explain or persuade. Thus it is said that 'authority is the form in which all truth reaches us in childhood'. A wider experience may entitle us to independent judgements, but authority, like duty, is ever at hand, and

> if through confidence misplaced
> We fail, thy saving arms, dread Power! around us cast.

Obedience, submission, implicit acceptance describe the state of mind correlative to this authority. In this sense, authority is contrasted with reason. Whenever a man adopts an opinion without himself going through the appropriate process of reasoning which would lead to that conclusion, but because it is presented to him complete by someone whom he thinks more competent than himself, his belief is said to be the work of authority. And, on the other side, whoever converses dogmatically, 'like a law-giver', forcing opinions into the minds of his audience, speaks as an authority. 'I am confident that the dead have some kind of existence,' says Socrates with unwonted dogmatism; and Simmias, wishing to pass from authority which merely constrains opinion to reason which persuades and enlightens, asks, 'Do you mean to go away and keep this belief to yourself, or will you let us share it with you?'[1]

Now, the ambiguity of this notion of authority seems to me this, that authority cannot be both external and coercive: if it be external, then it can be coercive in only a vague, metaphorical sense. For an external 'authority' can refer solely to the historical or psychological *cause* of belief, opinion or action, never to its whole *ground*, and it would be absurd to maintain that the power which actually compels a belief belongs merely to its cause.

[1] *Phaedo*, 63, c. *Republic*, 345, b. and Pater, *Plato and Platonism*, chapter vii.

This distinction between the causes or antecedents which produce a belief and the grounds or reason which alone sustain and justify one, is, I think, important. To believe a statement because we have been taught it, because a friend believes it or because the whole village believes it, is a common enough experience, but we are in error if we suppose that these causes, as such, are or can be the whole ground of any belief whatever. The cause of our belief that a certain man is guilty of murder may be the knowledge that he has been convicted in a court of law; the ground of this belief, however, is not the bare consciousness of the verdict, but a judgement we make about the whole body of evidence brought against him, or (failing a detailed acquaintance with that) an independent judgement, resting upon and guaranteed by our whole world of ideas, that those who have sifted the evidence are competent to arrive at a true conclusion. Or again, the ground of a belief in an historical fact is not that it is recorded by an historian, nor that it is asserted by a contemporary, nor that it is attested by an eye-witness, it is an independent judgement we make about the credibility of the fact proposed, by which we test these other, secondary witnesses and beside which they are no more than the causes of belief. Such a judgement may, indeed, involve a so-called interpretation of the 'fact', but we should remember that it is impossible to distinguish between what has 'come' to us and our 'interpretation' of it.[2] The ground of our belief that the Duke of Clarence was drowned in a butt of Marmsey is the credibility of the incident: had it been a butt of oysters we should, no doubt, have rejected it. The cause of a belief or action may, then, be spoken of as external, but belief or action which rests solely upon such a cause lacks any ground to sustain it, and consequently falls short of the nature of a belief or action; it is a bare abstraction. A merely external authority is, then, left hanging in the air; it is a cause severed from a ground. We may derive our opinions from this 'authority', but it is never the whole ground of these opinions, because the ground of any such opinion always contains some independent judgement about that 'authority'. We accept such an authority not on its own recommendation, but for reasons which lie outside its jurisdiction. And the correlative of this authority is a 'belief' which has a cause but no reason, or an 'action' which has a history but no justification; and it need scarcely be

___

[2] Hort, *The Way, the Truth, the Life*, p. 175.

remarked that such a 'belief' is utterly unrecognizable, and such an 'action' quite inconceivable. This authority refers to a mere aspect of some beliefs and actions, but has no reference whatever to any belief or action as a whole. And consequently, its coerciveness is confined to its arbitrary refusal to explain or persuade; whereas all that can be really coercive of an opinion or action is its whole ground. What compels me to believe is never the mere cause which produces the belief, but always the whole ground which sustains it. In short, this 'authority' is a vicious abstraction; if it be external, it cannot be itself coercive, and if it be not coercive I fail to understand in what sense it can be authoritative. We must look elsewhere for an unambiguous conception of authority.

Nor is the common notion of authority self-contradictory merely in this respect. For first, we ordinarily speak as if authority were a matter of *right*, and distinguish between a 'legitimate' authority and a usurpation of it, as if an authority required or could possess some external evidence of itself beyond the actual ability to coerce. Yet surely, that only can be authoritative which actually compels adhesion, and no claim or proclamation or air on the part of some person or thing can create authority where the power to sustain it is lacking. All authority is, as such, legitimate so long as it is really authoritative. And secondly, we speak of a 'limited authority', as if a person or thing could itself be really authoritative and at the same time owe allegiance elsewhere. That which actually compels obedience cannot, as such, be limited, for whatever was supposed to limit it would itself be the only really authoritative authority.

These, then, are some of the difficulties of the common notion, which must be overcome if we are to achieve a clear conception of authority. And in attempting this, let us consider the general character of whatever is actually authoritative, for our problem is not, what is the character of that which *claims* authority? but, what is the character of that which actually *exercises* authority?

I take it that only a measure of perversity which can expect no reply will question the supposition that coerciveness is inseparable from whatever is actually authoritative; that which does not itself actually compel belief or action, and from the command of which there is no appeal, is not in the full sense authoritative; and conversely, that which is really coercive of belief and action is the authority upon which they rest. If this be so, it follows that authority is never external, for we are never compelled by that which remains outside ourselves. The cause of a belief or action may be external, but its whole ground (of which the cause is a mere abstraction) is never external, and it is the whole ground which, in every case, is coercive. The cause of a soldier's action may be the command of his superior, which is external, but that which compels him to obey or disobey (for the authority of the one must be that of the other) is not the external command itself, but some judgement he makes, tacitly or explicitly, about the command; and such a judgement is in no sense external. Or again, that which compels us to hold a belief which was derived from some external source – a book, a person or a tradition – is not the 'authority' of that source (for it can in itself have none), but some judgement we make about its reliability, or indeed, a reason utterly unconnected with the source of the belief. The external cause of my belief that this earth is globular was, I suppose, a nursemaid or a kindergarten mistress, but I cannot pretend that the authority which now sustains this belief for me is in any way connected with that now long-forgotten cause. The 'authority' of what is external (the 'authority,' for example, of the expert) is, then, derivative and dependent, it has no power of its own to compel obedience and is consequently spurious.

Moreover, that which actually compels belief or action cannot itself be subject to any further and greater power, for that which is itself limited and derives its power from outside itself cannot be said itself to compel. To speak of the sanction of authority is to commit a pleonasm; an authority is always its own sanction. That which is authoritative is, thus, absolute and unlimited, not in the sense of embracing every detail, but because there can be no appeal from it. The real authority of all belief and action is that which can show itself to be absolute, irresponsible, self-supporting and inescapable.

Also, that which is authoritative is always single and indivisible: for a series of reasons which really compels a belief is the necessary foundation of that belief, and a foundation, as such, is always a unity. Thus, it is nonsense to say that the final authority of Christianity is to be found in 'history, reason and spiritual experience', or in 'the Scriptures and human reason',[3] for neither the Scriptures, nor history, nor spiritual

---

[3] I quote from the section on *Authority in Essays Catholic and Critical* (pp. 95, 119), which seems to me to have all the deficiencies usual to theological discussions of this subject.

experience (if it be isolated and externalized in this manner) are in themselves able to compel belief. They are the cause of many beliefs, but that upon which they depend, which itself compels and which is consequently the only true authority, is a judgement we make about their truth or value. The authority of a belief is its necessary ground, which is inconceivable except as a single whole; necessities, because we cannot distinguish between them, always constitute a unity.

In short, then, that which alone has power to coerce belief or action, and which is consequently the only final authority, is our world of ideas as a whole. It only is itself compelling and inescapable, because it is the ground of all belief and action. With a real authority there is no question whether or not we shall accept it, we have no choice in the matter, for an authority which we can escape is an imposter. An authority is not a person or institution whose experience we decide to accept and make use of where our own appears deficient, for such an 'authority' is secondary and compels not by its own but by a borrowed power; a real authority is the whole ground upon which our acceptance or rejection of anything is based. To have a belief it must be ours, and even if it were derived from some external source, that which actually compels us to hold it is the ground on which it has been accepted, that is, the whole world of ideas into which it has been fitted and in the light of which it has been understood and appropriated. The whole ground of whatever we accept or do is, then, the only real authority for its acceptance or performance. Nor is this true of adult life alone. Authority, in this sense, is not more the form in which truth reaches us in childhood than in old age: no belief was ever entertained, no action ever performed which was not based upon the authority of some ground which was more than a mere cause. And an absolute, compelling and at the same time external authority is as much a psychological curiosity as it is a logical monster. And finally, that which is really authoritative in belief or action, so far from standing in contrast to reason, *is* reason in the full sense of our world of ideas in so far as it is a coherent whole. So-called 'unreasonable' actions and 'superstitious' beliefs are not actions and beliefs which have no ground in a world of ideas (for such are impossible), but those the mere cause of which has usurped the place and name of the whole ground and are consequently random, capricious and unstable.[4]

[4] Wittgenstein, *Tractatus Logico-Philosophicus*, 1361, 5. 'Der Glaube au den Kausalnexus ist der Aberglaube.'

I turn now to the second question: What do we mean by the state? It is perhaps natural that one should be most critical of one's own subject of study, and I venture to think that the prospects of political thought today are darker even than those of theology. For the theory of politics has fallen on evil days, its ideas are for the most part misappropriated, its words mere jargon, and it is now too far gone in decay to allow of any sudden rejuvenation. And my attempt to answer this question about the state will, I fear, be inconclusive where I have paid too great attention to the traditional prejudices of political thinking, and obscure where I have attempted to stand clear of the familiar wreckage of dead controversies which we spend our time picking over.

'It may seem curious', says a writer on politics, 'that so great and obvious a fact as the state should be the object of quite conflicting definitions, yet such certainly is the case.'[5] And in this double assumption that the state is an 'obvious fact' and that different conceptions of it merely and necessarily conflict, lies, I think, one of the radical defects of modern political thinking. The first has fostered a perverted realism which mistakes any persistent fancy or useful fiction for a fact, the second reduces all argument to an *ignoratio elenchi*, and together they have obstructed all attempts to work out a clear and complete conception of the state. For the state is not an 'obvious fact' (in that sense there are no facts), it is a conception which we may permit ourselves to call a fact only when we have made it clear to ourselves and complete in itself. That the literature of political thinking contains many different conceptions of the state is not, I think, remarkable: of nothing with which the human mind has ever occupied itself is there but a single conception. What is important, however, is that we should understand the relationship of these different conceptions. Some writers assume that they are bare alternatives and invite us to choose which we will,[6] but pluralism run to seed is not an engaging spectacle. Others take them to be merely conflicting,[7] but to set one against another is not the way to get the truth out of ideas. Others again imagine a complete conception of the state to be constructed from the contributions of lesser and different conceptions,[8] but this also is a relationship

[5] MacIver, *The Modern State*, p. 3.
[6] Laski, *The Study of Politics*.
[7] MacIver, *Op. cit.*
[8] Barker, *The Study of Political Science*.

foreign to the nature of ideas; a complete conception was never achieved by adding together conceptions in themselves imperfect. In place of these, however, the view I wish to suggest is that a complete conception of the state is one which supersedes all others and beside which they appear neither as possible alternatives, nor as contradictions nor as contributions, but as abstractions to be supplanted. Each conception of the state, however limited, may have its use; to compare them is irrelevant, to set them against one another futile, to add them together impossible. The legal conception of the state cannot be said to be alternative to or to conflict with any other so long as it confines itself to its own province, any more than a mathematical conception of the world can be said to conflict with a moral conception. But if we are determined to arrive at a complete conception of the state, these others will afford us no assistance, they are obstacles to be overcome, abstract points of view to be superseded. And we shall discover the 'fact', the state itself, only when we have achieved such a conception as this. It is impossible to examine all the conceptions of the state which have been devised, but in order to make what suggestions I can about the character of the state I propose now to consider a few of the more common conceptions of its nature and to show how what is less adequate yields to and is superseded by what is more adequate.

The state, it is said, is a piece of territory. This, geographical, conception of the state will require but little argument on my part to show its imperfection. Indeed, those who propose it usually do so in what they take to be a less categorical form, asserting that the state is *at least* a piece of territory, and thus themselves reveal the indigence of their conception. For, if the mere possession of territory, taken alone, does not give an adequate conception of the state, territory is no more than a symptom of the state's existence, and a conception which includes mere symptoms includes what it has no business to recognize. 'But', it will be said, 'the possession of territory enters into the legal conception of the state.' Yet, what does this suggest more than that a legal conception is an adequate, arbitrary, abstract, agreed conception, and not one we can recognize beyond its own world? The legal conception of the state, like legal personality and legal responsibility, is an agreed fiction which must be superseded before we can achieve the complete fact.

The state is a collection of persons. This also falls short of the complete conception we are looking for and must consequently be superseded. Persons in some sense are necessary to the state, and some kind of relationship must exist between them before they can be spoken of as members of the state, but we have not achieved the full conception of the state until the persons it comprises are concrete and not abstract and the relationship between them concrete and not abstract. For the nature of things is correlative with the relationship which exists between them, and a mere collection is possible only to abstract mathematical units. A collection of legal 'persons' may constitute a legal 'state', and a collection of economic 'persons' an economic state, but such states are as abstract as their constituents.

The state is the secular whole, or persons organized for secular purposes. This is an important conception because it is the theoretical belief of most Englishmen; nevertheless it is, I think, imperfect. For the constituents of a secular whole must be 'secular persons', and since merely secular persons are as abstract as merely legal or economic persons, the whole into which they might be imagined to organize themselves is equally abstract. Were the state the mere secular whole it would be a vicious abstraction, something which results from an arbitrary analysis of any community as we know it and exists nowhere outside that analysis. This is not a question of the so-called establishment of religion, or of the so-called 'modern' state; society as it organizes itself apart from God is an abstraction, and the state cannot be identified with this secular whole without becoming an abstraction, and a conception which ends in an abstraction requires no further evidence of its imperfection. The conception of the state as the mere secular whole is imperfect because it leads not to a fact but to a fiction. And if such a truth may be spoken of as established, this was certainly established by Dante in the *De Monarchia*.

'The state is the political machinery of government in a community,'[9] or the political whole. This I suppose is the commonest practical conception of the state; 'the state', says a popular writer on the subject, 'is concerned with those social relations which express themselves by means of government';[10] but we have yet to discover whether it gives us a fact or

[9] G. D. H. Cole, *Self-Government in Industry*, p. 71.
[10] Laski, *Authority in the Modern State*, p. 26.

an abstraction. And indeed, we need enquire only whether persons as government sees them are complete, or whether, like legal persons, they are abstract, to perceive the defects of this conception of the state. Men as governed are abstractions, for no man is merely what the government as such thinks he is; and consequently the political whole which such 'persons' constitute is an abstraction also. Government activity is not a self-explanatory activity; its end is always beyond the perfection of itself; it deals with an aspect of life, never with the whole of it. An aspect of almost all social relations is expressed by means of government, but no single, concrete social relationship can ever be expressed in this manner. If the state be no more than the government or the community as organized for merely political purposes, then it is a bare abstraction, a fiction and not a fact. The detailed nature and limits of government do not here concern us, all that is necessary now is that we should see clearly that the conception of the state which identifies it with the mere political whole is only less barren than that which identified it with the secular or the economic whole.

Where, then, shall we turn for a fuller conception of the state? If it is to be a concrete fact, the state must be self-subsistent, something which carries with it the explanation of itself and requires to be linked on to no more comprehensive whole in order to be understood. And it appears to me that nothing fulfils these conditions save the social whole which is correlative to individuals who are complete and living persons; or, in other words, the totality in an actual community which satisfies the whole mind of the individuals who comprise it. All that falls short of this is an abstraction which requires this to explain it. Government and law, economic, religious, intellectual and every other activity and aspect of social life find their explanation in this totality; it is to perfect this, and not merely themselves, that they exist.

I cannot now enter into all the implications of this conception of the state, and indeed I do not pretend that they are all as clear to me as I should wish, but I would like to meet three of the commonest misapprehensions concerning it. First, its opponents sometimes represent it as the apotheosis of the political status quo, the identification of government, or the political whole, with all that satisfies the mind of complete and concrete persons, but it is not difficult to recognize this as a total misrepresentation. The state is not the government, it is the social whole which government implies and requires for its explanation; for to explain a thing is to think of it in terms of the whole which it implies. We must forget altogether that anyone has been so foolish as to think that society as politically organized is more than an abstraction. Secondly, it is said that this view fails to distinguish between society and the state and is, therefore, at best a mere confusion, at worst pernicious logomachy. But it seems to me that if we separate the 'state' (politically organized society) from society, we have, on the one side, mere government, political organization for its own sake, which is not only (as Schopenhauer said) the apotheosis of philistinism, but a sheer abstraction which exists nowhere; and on the other side, a society without organization, which again is an abstraction and nowhere to be found in the concrete world. The separation of the state from society not merely fails to give us a clearer conception of the state and of society, but ensures that we shall have no conception of either full enough to dignify with the name of 'fact'. And thirdly, it will be asked, 'If the state is all that satisfies the whole needs of complete persons, *where*, then, is the state?' And I can reply only that the state exists insofar as such a satisfaction exists, and wherever that satisfaction is found, there is the state. The state comprises whatever affords that satisfaction, it comprises nothing which does not afford it, and is the totality or unity of conditions which fulfils the needs of complete persons. And no one who has grasped the conception will require to be shown the *locus* of a totality, or suppose it to be non-existent because he cannot designate it.

In short, the view I have been recommending is this. The state is a conceptions which, like all conceptions, may be called a concrete fact only when it is full enough to be complete in itself. Many conceptions of the state are defective because they result not in facts, but fictions such as society as politically, or ecclesiastically, or industrially organized. The limitations of such conceptions as these make them useful in practical life, but if we set out to construct a complete conception, these and their like must disappear. We are driven from the more abstract to the less abstract until we reach the complete. And when the gods appear, the half-gods disappear. Thus 'society as politically organized' is less abstract than 'secular society', because the political whole more nearly supplies to our complete needs than the secular whole; the merely political man is more complete than the merely secular man. But the conception which alone achieves the realm of fact is that which views the state as the necessary totality or identity which the *prima facie* variety and difference of human life implies. All activity directed towards the satisfaction of the needs of concrete persons is state activity. Government frequently contributes to this satisfaction, law is the regulation of a certain limited aspect of it, the Church (whether or not established), the trade union and the family are its organs. Anything less than this is an abstraction; sometimes, like the abstractions of law and economics, useful; at others, like many of the abstractions of so-called political science, serving only to obscure the truth.

This does not mean that the state is anything other than its members – that is a subject which I have not discussed and which I think it impossible to discuss until we have abandoned the moral and legal conception of the individual as that which is isolated, for a more concrete conception which takes him to be that which is complete.

There remains now to consider the third question; where, then, is the authority of the state? The reply is, of course, implied in what I have said about the nature of authority and the character of the state, but I wish to consider two answers which have hitherto found favour among writers on politics.

The authority of the state, or the sovereign power in the state, it is said, is the government, and the voice of government is law. The final authority of the state is the legislative authority. Now, we have seen that a real authority is something which we cannot go behind, something from which there is no possibility of appeal, something irresponsible, inescapable and complete in itself, and we have now to enquire whether government and law fulfil these conditions. From one point of view, it is true, the legislative authority is absolute and irresponsible – from the point of view of the practising lawyer and the administrator. A judge, a lawyer or an administrator does not enquire whether a statute be just or expedient; he asks, merely, what it says. It is something to which he appeals as an absolute and inescapable authority.[11] The law, for him, can do no wrong. But this, again, is not a concrete 'fact', it is merely a useful legal fiction. Everyone, save the actual administrator as such, may and does question the justice or expedience of the acts of

[11] It might be argued that the legislative authority in America occupies no such position as this, but the argument would not, of course, affect the point at issue here.

the legislative authority. It is not a power from which there is no appeal, for laws can be changed and governments overthrown. It is legally irresponsible because it is the sole creator of law, but it is always responsible to another and wider tribunal – the moral and political opinions of its subjects. Government, indeed, as we all know, is sometimes not much better than the conversion of the opinions of idiots into laws; as Montaigne says, 'there is nothing so much, nor so grossly, nor so ordinarily faulty as the laws'; and no matter what its particular character be, it always draws its power from a source outside itself. So then, the point of view from which government and the law can be said, as such, to embody the authority of the state is limited and abstract, and their so-called 'authority' is derivative and not absolute, a legal fiction and not a fact. Some writers on politics today are exerting themselves to deprive the mere legislative power of the sovereign position which they imagine it to have held in the past and think it holds, for the most part, now; but their efforts seem to me wide of the mark. For no government, as such, was ever a strictly sovereign power, or had ever a more than derivative 'authority'. The nature of government excludes the possibility of it being itself the real authority which actually compels any belief or action.

Now, the traditional escape from the anomalies of this notion of the authority of the state is by means of a conception in terms of consent. 'The supreme power', says Locke, 'remains with the people'; the authority which is behind government, which gives power to law and to which any appeal from these must be made, is the consent of the people, the will, if not of all, at least of the majority. Yet this appears to me scarcely more satisfactory than the notion it was designed to supersede. For, in the first place, consent can never create or maintain authority; authority is never authoritative because it is consented to. That which actually compels us to act or believe is something inherent in the character of the belief or action, is the necessary ground upon which it rests, and not our consent to it, which is never more than a cause. Mere consent may be given or withheld, but whatever is really authoritative is absolute and independent of our acceptance or recognition: consent itself requires an authority upon which to rest. And secondly, what is this 'people' whose will as such is supposed to be the authority behind government? It is, in fact, never more than a class in the community, a fluctuating and elusive majority, wholly without the characteristics of authority – absoluteness, self-subsistence and irresponsibility. The *volonté de tous*, as Rousseau long ago insisted, is itself in no sense authoritative. The people, as such, is never the sovereign power in the state.

Where, then, *is* the authority of the state? Where is this absolute, irresponsible, inescapable power vested, which alone (we have seen) can be called an authority? If it be vested neither in the government as such, nor in the people as such, is it not, perhaps, a phantom which has lured us from the path of fact? This, or some variant of it, is, I suppose, the conclusion reached by the dominant faction in political thinking today, but that should not, I think, deter us from rejecting it: it is, in fact, no conclusion at all. For nothing is more certain than that no belief was ever entertained, no action ever performed which was not based upon some absolute and inescapable authority. And the only authority which corresponds to this description is (we have seen) the whole ground upon which a belief or action rests. If actual authority belong only to the whole ground of a belief or action, if such an authority is absolute and inescapable, and if (further) the only conception of the state which escapes the taint of abstraction is that which considers it to be the totality of necessary conditions which fulfils the needs of concrete persons, the whole ground of their actions and beliefs, then the authority of the state can reside nowhere save in the state itself as such. The authority of the state is not mere government and law, nor is it founded upon a contract or any other form of the consent of the people, but resides solely in the completeness of the satisfaction which the state itself affords to the needs of concrete persons. Apart from its completeness, the state has no authority, for that only is authoritative, in the full sense, which is itself complete. Of this authority, and of no other, can it be said: *Non est potestas super terram quae comparetur ei.*

THE AUTHORITY OF THE STATE

Sir,

I hope I shall not be thought impertinent if I make certain comments on the article by Mr Oakeshott on 'The Authority of the State' in the Conference Number of the *Modern Churchman*. (a) On p. 318 Mr Oakeshott confuses authority with the grounds for accepting authority. (b) On p. 323 Mr Oakeshott puts forward the desideratum for the state that it shall need 'to be linked on to the more comprehensive whole in order to be understood . . .'. He speaks of the social whole, which is correlated to individuals who are complete and living persons. This is to establish an ideal, as Hegel did, for the state (an ideal to which no actual state has, I think it can be argued, conformed, since states are not little-minded communities in basis). If, however, we are talking about the ideal community, Mr Oakeshott gives no reason why it should be limited in extent to the national state. He does not appear to advance beyond the expedient grounds dogmatically affirmed by Bosanquet as final ones. (c) On p. 323 again he rightly (although tautologically?) insists that a society must have organization. He also asserts that a mere government is a sheer abstraction: I do not know what this means, but calling 'the state organization regarded as government' as distinct from the citizen body organized by its government and laws is not an abstraction. Here, however, if we grant this point, it by no means follows in logic or in anthropology that a society, if it is to be organized, must be organized as a state, under state government. Emphatically societies otherwise organized than as states (national states?) are and have been 'facts.' Because Mr Oakeshott happens to like this historical form of organization it certainly does not follow that it is the only possible one or the only ideal one or the only one which can be 'dignified with the name of fact' (need facts be dignified?). There is the ink of the old Bosanquetian confidence trick: 'accept my values, and you will accept my conclusions' – of course. . . .

I write this not as mere carping but because the fourteen conclusions from this very Bosanquetian and but too popular but very vulnerable argument seems to me to be most dangerous – as has been insisted now for some years past by at least one school.

Have you seen the little book on politics by Beman and others of the Life and Liberty group? It has been sent me by them and, from the glance I have had time to take at it, seems quite good.

G. E. G. CATLIN

Cornell University, USA

THE AUTHORITY OF THE STATE

REPLY OF MR OAKESHOTT

SIR,

(a) I am aware that it is not unusual to distinguish between an 'authority' and the ground of it, but since this seemed to me to involve a confusion of thought I was forced to reject it. What I had hoped to show was that a person, doctrine, etc, distinguished from its logical ground, cannot be called an 'authority' because it is never authoritative. An 'authority' separated from its ground is not authoritative because it is a base abstraction, the mere aspect of an authority which happens to touch us. A policeman is not himself authoritative, but draws his authority from the law; while the law, as such, is not itself authoritative because it also, if it have feet of its own, still requires some ground upon which to stand them. That alone is itself authoritative which (like reason, in the sense in which I used the word) stands upon itself. The isolated aspect which touches us is no more itself authoritative than is an isolated statement itself true, or an isolated act itself moral.

(b) Though the view I put forward owed much to Hegel and Bosanquet, I do not think I should be held responsible for their line of argument, which I regard as in many respects fallacious and which I did not myself use or refer to. And while I should welcome a critic who aimed at correcting my argument of fallacy, I find it difficult to know what to say to one who merely misread it in the light of writers to whom I made and intended no reference whatever.

Nowhere in my paper have I said anything which might lead a reader to suppose me to be speaking of an 'ideal' state. Nor does it seem to me necessary to regard as 'ideal' all conceptions of the state other than the ordinary historico-legal conception. The moral conception of personality is not 'ideal' because it is different from the legal conception.

And the conclusion which might properly be drawn from my argument is not that the 'national state' (which I never mentioned) is the 'ideal', but that this historico-legal conception of the state is not only one among many, but is less complete than that which I recommended. It is absurd to assume that the word 'state' can have have and ought to have a single meaning; all that is required is that it should have a single and intelligible meaning in any one argument. What I meant by it was neither something merely 'ideal', nor anything in the phenomenal world. And to assail my argument on the basis of either of these meanings is to commit at once the *ignoratio elenchi* I spoke of on p. 319.

(c) In saying that mere government, as such, is an abstraction I meant that it is a mere aspect of social experience, inseparable from the whole, and not itself a self-complete fact. Society in its exclusively governmental aspect is an abstraction for the same reason as the purely numerical aspect of a collection of pictures is an abstraction.

And so far from indicating a preference for the 'national state' as the best form of organization for all communities, or thinking of it as the only possible form of organization, I nowhere used the word 'state' in this sense, and was careful to point out that I regarded such use as a merely legitimate technicality – analogous to the lawyer's use of 'real' in the expression 'real property', or to the 'universe' of the physicist. And since it was not I who introduced the subject of the 'ideal state,' I need scarcely say that my conclusions do not depend upon any esoteric 'values' of my own. But, of course, if an argument which makes no appeal to the writings of others is to be disposed of by the attribution of a name – Erastian, Hegelian, 'old Bosanquetian' – there must be an end to all rational discussion. And so far as I understand it myself, I had not conceived it more possible for my argument to be called Erastian than pink or mammalian.

Michael Oakeshott

Gonville and Caius College, Cambridge

6

THE CLAIMS OF POLITICS

1939

So many good people nowadays take an interest in politics and even arrive at some kind of political action that the view that it is the duty of everyone to do something of the sort has become almost a commonplace, and not to recognize the claim of politics is taken to indicate some defect of character or sensibility. Nevertheless, this alleged obligation of everyone to take part in immediate political activity is, I believe, a gross delusion; at best it is based upon a perverted social sense, at worst upon a false scale of values. I leave on one side such quasi-political activity as the exercise of the vote and the informal discussion of political questions. Most intelligent people will wish to be informed about what is happening in the world of politics and may perhaps wish to cast a vote. The more difficult question is the alleged obligation of everyone to take some more extended and more active part in politics.

Now, I take it that political action could reasonably be considered a universal duty if either of two conditions were satisfied. If political activity were the only adequate expression of a sensibility for the communal interests of a society or of mankind, or if it were incomparably the most important and most effective expression of such a sensibility – in either of these cases it might fairly be held that a universal duty exists to take part in it. Let us consider what truth there may be in either of these views about the nature of political action.

For any sensitive and educated person to feel that he takes little or no part in the promotion of the collective interests of his society or of mankind may provoke in him a sense of having failed to perform one of his duties. And the belief that those who take part in the direction or administration of the social or political system have the monopoly of what is called social service, that public activity is the sole genuine and adequate expression of public spirit, leads such a person to suppose that his whole duty remains unfulfilled unless, besides going about what he thinks of as his business, he takes an active part in the public affairs of his society. In the less sensitive the same neglect coupled with the same belief leads to the less creditable feeling of being outside the main stream of the life of their time. But it is a false belief, disastrous at once to the life of a society and to the conduct of its affairs. Just as the similar belief that the true, unhindered service of God was possible only to members of a religious order or officials of the Church (that is, to those who made a profession of it) promoted a false and irreligious division between those who were called to serve God and those who were not, and gave a false importance to the former, so this belief about social service promotes the erroneous view that some activity is disconnected from the communal life of a society and gives a false importance to the activity of those who engage in public life. Our sense of the unity of social life degenerates; and by elevating unnaturally one form of communal activity, other forms, no less communal, are unnaturally depressed. But the truth is that nothing we do is unconnected with the life of our society, no activity is private in the sense of being without its place or context in the corporate social life, and no man who feels it his duty to take a part in the promotion of the communal interests of his society need consider himself to have failed merely because he has not entered the world of politics. The activity of a music-hall artist is no less certainly connected with the common life of his society than that of a Prime Minister or functionary, personal relationships are not less communal than public and legal relationships, and a sense of public duty which is satisfied only by some form of public activity is a sense which rests upon and helps to perpetuate an illusory division in the life of a society. Our choice, then, lies not between a life exclusively devoted to merely private interests and one connected with the communal life of our society, but between a life which has its place either here or there in the common life, a life which touches the life and interests of our society either in this way or in that.

But the defence of this alleged obligation of everyone to take part in immediate political action may be conducted on different lines. Instead of asserting that such action is a universal duty because it is the only genuine and adequate expression of a public spirit, it is suggested that the kind of communal activity we call political is of superior importance to any other kind, that it is incontestably the most effective expression of a sensibility for the common interests of a society. But there is, I believe, little or no truth in this suggestion. Politics is a highly specialized and abstracted form of communal activity; it is conducted on the surface of the life of a society and except on rare occasions makes remarkably small impression below that surface. If politics were the continuous consideration and reconsideration of the life and order of a society from the bottom upwards, and if political activity involved the continuous recreation of the communal life, then, no doubt, for good or for ill, it would be highly important; but it is not. A political system is primarily for the protection and occasional modification of a recognized legal and social order. It is not self-explanatory; its end and meaning lie beyond itself in the social whole to which it belongs, a social whole already determined by law and custom and tradition, none of which is the creation of political activity. Political activity may have given us Magna Carta and the Bill of Rights, but it did not give us the contents of these documents, which came from a stratum of social thought far too deep to be influenced by the actions of politicians. A political system presupposes a civilization; it has a function to perform in regard to that civilization, but it is a function mainly of protection and to a minor degree of merely mechanical interpretation and expression. The things political activity can achieve are often valuable, but I do not believe that they are ever the most valuable things in the communal life of a society. A limitation of view, which appears so clear and practical, but which amounts to little more than a mental fog, is inseparable from political activity. A mind fixed and callous to all subtle distinctions, emotional and intellectual habits become bogus from repetition and lack of examination, unreal loyalties, delusive aims, false significances are what political action involves. And this is so, not because the politically active are under the necessity of persuading the mentally obtuse before their activity can succeed; the spiritual callousness involved in political action belongs to its character, and follows from the nature of what can be achieved politically. Political action involves mental vulgarity, not merely because it entails the concurrence and support of those who are mentally vulgar, but because of the false simplification of human life implied in even the best of its purposes. There are some, no doubt, who feel the need for the 'illusion of affairs', and to these the superior importance of political activity, even in normal circumstances, will appear beyond question. But it is little more than a personal and psychological importance, and cannot be made the basis of a universal duty. In normal times, then, the superior importance of political activity over all other expressions of sensibility for the communal interests of a society, cannot, I think, be maintained. But at times of political crisis, when a society seems to be in danger of destruction, and when the work of protection appears to be more important than anything else, there is a special temptation to believe in the overwhelmingly superior importance of political activity. Nevertheless, this also is a temptation to be avoided. The work of protection is never of primary importance; and when, in times of political crisis, it appears to be so, that is merely because, in the absence or poverty of creative activity, protection has usurped the place of recreation. On occasion a society may be preserved and may survive by means of political action, but to make it live requires a social activity of a different and more radical character; and its life is as often threatened by political success as by political failure.

Political activity as I understand it, then, is neither the only adequate expression, nor the overwhelmingly most important expression of a sensibility for the communal interests of a society or of mankind. And consequently I do not think that there is a duty for everyone to take part in it. And if it is found that there is a necessary service to society which can be performed only on the condition of an abstention from political activity, then it may be said that those who are capable of performing such a service have a duty not to engage in politics. Nothing I have said should be taken to mean that I think political action is a wholly valueless expression of a sensibility for the communal interests of a society; in my view it is a legitimate expression, and one which it is impossible for a society to go without. It is probably true that any man who can be strongly tempted to give himself up to political activity belongs to the world of politics, and he will not go wrong if he follows his genius. He will use his intelligence to reflect on questions of political importance; as a writer he will become a publicist. In action, if he is prudent and lucky, he may be successful. He will retain his fundamental views and opinions almost unchanged, being without time or inclination to examine them afresh; and he may take on the appearance of a leader.

But in every society there are, I believe, some for whom political activity would be a perversion of their genius, a disloyalty to themselves, not because they have little or no part in the promotion of the communal interests of their society, but because their part is one which it is essential that a society shall have performed and which it is difficult if not impossible to combine with political activity. And among them, I believe, are those whose genius and interest lies in literature, in art and in philosophy.

The grounds on which I distinguish this section of society from all others in respect of political activity are clear to me. Their business is with the values which are the real life and character of a society. They are not (what they are sometimes called) the guardians of the values of society. Every society has its values, but if they are *guarded* at all, it is the politically active who do it. A society requires not only that its civilization should be guarded, but that it should be recreated. And the genius of the poet and the artist and to a lesser extent of the philosopher is to create and recreate the values of their society. In them a society becomes conscious and critical of itself, of its whole self; just as, in the politically active, it becomes conscious of its political self. The last corruption that can visit a society is a corruption of its consciousness, and from this the politically active cannot protect it. If a society is to be saved from a corrupt consciousness it will be saved not by having its values and its civilization protected, but by knowing itself and having its values recreated. Indeed, political activity involves a corruption of consciousness from which a society has continuously to be saved. To ask the poet and the artist to provide a programme for political or other social action, or an incentive or an inspiration for such action, is to require them to be false to their own genius and to deprive society of a necessary service. What they provide is action itself, but in another and deeper sphere of consciousness. It is not their business to suggest a political remedy for political defects, but to provide an actual remedy for more fundamental defects by making a society conscious of its own character. The emotional and intellectual integrity and insight for which they stand is something foreign to the political world, foreign not merely in fact, but in essence. This integrity and insight cannot be introduced into that world without changing their character; and to attempt to introduce them makes a chaos of what is otherwise a restricted but nevertheless ordered view. It is not their business to come out of a retreat, bringing with them some superior wisdom, and enter the world of political activity, but to stay where they are, remain true to their genius, which is to mitigate a little their society's ignorance of itself. This is the truth of the neglected half-truth that the artist and the poet and the philosopher are and should remain separated from 'the world'; not because they have no part in the promotion of the communal interests of mankind, but because to be free from the world is the condition of their contribution. Societies, in fact, are led from behind, and for those capable of leadership to give themselves up to political activity is to break away from their true genius. And a society in which this becomes common will, in a short while, be a society without leaders, a society ignorant of itself and without the power of recreating itself. And this is true not less in times of political crisis than in others. Culture, it is true, is indebted most to the politically weakened periods of history; but in a society which circumstances encourage to embrace an exclusively political view, it has still its part and its friends their duty.

7

SCIENTIFIC POLITICS

1947

I

This is a book,[1] good enough to wish it were better, and profound enough to wish it were more lucid. It argues courageously against so much that is false but still accepted as incontestably true, and consequently is sure to need some defence against the confident smiles of the pundits of error; but it requires, also, some defence against itself. Its title is unfortunate, its argument at times confused, and its style unhappy. Yet, with all its faults, there is so much to be learned from it that no intelligent reader will allow himself to be put off by its eccentricities.

The observation from which it begins is the deplorable lack of success of modern politics, 'the failure of our society to understand, and to cope with, the political problems which the age poses, especially on the international scene'. This, to the theorists who think they and their pupils are doing fine and that it is only mischievous criticism which prevents them doing even better, will appear a strange piece of misobservation. But anyone without a theory to defend will find it near enough to the mark. Nevertheless, this does not exactly represent the starting-place of Professor Morgenthau's thought. He writes sometimes as if he knew of a golden age in the past when European society was strikingly more successful in dealing with its political problems than it now appears to be, but what he really wants us to understand is something less fanciful. It is, that success in politics is unavoidably sporadic and un-

---

[1] Hans J. Morgenthau, *Scientific Man Versus Power Politics* (1946).

certain, something which has to be achieved from day to day and is never complete or unqualified, and that the aggravated failure of modern politics represents, not necessarily a greater absolute failure, but a failure relatively more humiliating because it follows upon a far more extended promise of success than any other age has ever been offered. 'Two moods', he says, 'determine the attitude of our civilization to the social world: confidence in the power of reason, as represented by modern science, to solve the social problems of our age, and despair at the ever renewed failure of scientific reason to solve them.' This confidence he believes to be misplaced; it is, indeed, the great illusion of modern politics. And the despair is now desperate because it does not spring from disillusion, but merely from a frustration of hopes still entertained.

2

Let us consider first Professor Morgenthau's characterization of the belief. Since the seventeenth century, observation and reflection have convinced us that the natural or physical world can be made intelligible in terms of generalized forms of behaviour. And even if these generalizations are in constant need of revision and restatement (and even if research and reflection are unable to show why these and not other laws should prevail in the physical world), the increasing mastery we have over the physical world confirms to some extent the accuracy of our understanding of it. The success which has attended this attempt to understand the world of nature led to the supposition that the social world, the world of human activity and suffering, could be understood in precisely the same manner, and that (on the basis of this understanding) it could be mastered and controlled. And since the voices raised in criticism of this supposition were neither loud nor very firm, it was not long before the hypothesis became a hope, the hope a faith, and the faith a philosophy.

Professor Morgenthau holds that this belief may be described, alternatively, as the belief that scientific understanding is able to comprehend and, at least potentially, to solve all social problems (a belief which he calls 'scientism'), or as the belief that the social world is susceptible of understanding and control by 'reason' or 'the rational faculties of man' (a belief which he calls 'rationalism'). And the project which sprang from this belief he describes, alternatively, as 'science of politics', or as 'rational politics'.

There is no doubt that some such belief as this has long been entertained by European writers and that it has even become the common assumption of most of our political activity. But I am by no means certain that Professor Morgenthau has provided us with an accurate description of it. I think, first of all, that it is an over-simplification of the situation to see it as European society led by the successes of scientific enquiry to embrace a belief in the omni-competence of the scientific understanding. It is true that this is how it has appeared to many of the progenitors of a 'science of society'. But the pursuit of scientific enquiry and the theory of scientific enquiry called 'scientism' are not the same thing. Indeed, the second is a corruption of the first; 'scientism' is a superstition about scientific enquiry. And this difference is obscured when Professor Morgenthau attributes to 'scientism' the achievements of scientific enquiry about the physical world, and to scientific enquiry the role of having misled the world with regard to its own character. The belief, real and influential enough in the modern world, which Professor Morgenthau wants to bring before us is not the faith that the natural scientist has in his own methods of enquiry, nor even the belief (in J. S. Mill's words) that 'the methods of physical science are the proper models for political', but the belief that the problems of practical politics are, in the strict sense, scientific problems. And it is unfortunate that he often obscures his object by injudicious attacks upon scientific enquiry itself.

A parallel defect appears in his description of the belief he has in mind as the belief that the social world is susceptible of being understood by human reason and controlled according to the deliverances of human reason. What he really has in mind is not this, but a belief about the nature and scope of rational understanding which, on the one hand, confines it to the promulgation of abstract general propositions and, on the other hand, extends its relevance to the whole of human life – a doctrine which may be called 'rationalism'. And there is as much difference between rational enquiry and 'rationalism' as there is between scientific enquiry and 'scientism', and it is a difference of the same kind. Moreover, it is important that a writer who wishes to contest the excessive claims of 'rationalism' should observe the difference, because if he fails to do so he will not only be liable to self-contradiction (for his argument

99

will itself be nothing if it is not rational), but also he will make himself appear the advocate of irrationality, which is going further than he either needs or intends to go.

I have said that Professor Morgenthau really means to oppose, not scientific enquiry, but 'scientism' in politics, and not rationality, but 'rationalism' in politics, not merely because I think he ought to mean this, but because (in spite of the frequent confusion of his argument) there is plenty in his book to show that he can recognize these differences. What he has failed to do is to make his reader appreciate them at every turn in his argument, and we leave him with the impression that he has not detected the root of rationalism in politics.

3

He is on firmer ground when he turns from the characterization of the belief to the task of illustrating the appearance of the belief in the teachings of politicians and writers on politics. He shows convincingly that the ground and presupposition of all those beliefs and projects which are comprehensively and generally known as 'liberalism' are rationalism and scientism. Of course liberalism has to share these presuppositions with other systems of political thought but liberalism remains the most complete expression of these doctrines. This project of a science of politics is, indeed, the common ground of all that is most characteristic of modern politics. It is the common ground of both the achievements and the failures of modern politics, because it is the project which determines what is attempted. The belief that politics, at their best, are the science of the arrangement and improvement of human societies in accordance with certain abstract ideals which are taken to be absolute in value and universal in application, the belief that the problems of the organization of a society are scientific problems (that political conflict can be resolved into scientific controversy), the belief that politics are (or should be) 'social engineering' – these have been the main (though not exclusive) inspiration of political activity in Western Europe for the last two hundred years. They have inspired many great achievements: the supersession of violence by cooperative endeavour in many fields of human activity, and the whole movement for social and educational reform. And, not less surely, they have given us the ideas and ideals which determine our present political enterprises: that economics can and should replace politics, that the ideal of government is the administration of things and not the government of people, that the solution of every social and political problem lies in the discovery of an administrative technique, that all crime is a disease for which a cure can be found, that the risks and uncertainties of both political and commercial bargaining can be replaced by the certainty of rational calculation, that (in short) it is only our ignorance of the universal causes of human activity which stands between us and a society incomparably better ordered, more just and more prosperous than any human society that has yet existed. Perhaps it is in the sphere of international relationships that the project of a science of politics has made itself most clear. 'After rationalist philosophy, in its liberal manifestation, had passed successfully its domestic trial, the general idea of extending those same principles to the international field was transformed into a concrete political programme to be put to the test of actual realization.' From Grotius to the United Nations a continuous attempt has been made to demonstrate Bentham's proposition that 'nations are associates not rivals in the grand social enterprise', and to elaborate the principles of a science of peace. And Professor Morgenthau is an acute, if at times one-sided and inconsequent, guide for anyone wishing to follow the trail of this enterprise: he does not distinguish real moral achievements (such as they are) from rationalist aspirations and projects, but he knows an illusion when he sees one.

Now, before we go on to consider the reasons Professor Morgenthau gives for believing that the faith that has inspired this project of a science of politics is illusory, there are two further points to be considered with regard to his account of the nature of this faith and its manifestations. First, the reader will be disappointed if he looks in his essay for a genuinely historical account of the manifestations of this faith: Professor Morgenthau is, in fact, no historian. The historical springs of the faith remain a mystery, and the circumstances of its appearance and propagation are never properly considered. We are left with what appears to be a remarkable and unaccountable aberration of the human mind. This is unfortunate, because, while the faith has been detected and examined by other writers, what we are waiting for is a genuinely historical account of the circumstances of its emergence. And secondly, Professor Morgenthau's uncertain grasp of the root principles of the rationalist faith are revealed in his treatment of Fascism. This he identifies as a reaction against the prevailing enterprise, a rejection of rationalism and liberalism, and for no better reason than because this is what its prophets represented it as, and because of the anti-rational strain in its doctrines. Fascism *tout court* is, of course, something that exists only in the mind of the doctrinaire communist; it is an idol of propaganda. But if by Fascism is meant the lately defeated regime in Germany, then it may be observed that it represented anything but a reaction against rationalist politics. The so-called 'liberal' beliefs and practices which it rejected are precisely those which conflict with the characteristic liberal project of a science of politics, and are, indeed, not liberal at all, but of a far more ancient lineage in European politics. What Fascism rejected was something which Germany and the continent generally enjoyed only fitfully and never understood, the institutions and values of parliamentary government; what it represented was something that Germany and the continent understood very well − rationalistic politics. However, it is a mistake to get oneself involved in an argument about the nature of German Fascism, because it is difficult, if not impossible, to distinguish between those beliefs and practices which were designed *ad hoc* to promote victory in a projected war against the rest of the world, and those which may have a less purely temporary significance.

4

The faith stands before us with tolerable distinctness, the faith in a science of politics, the enterprise of converting politics into 'social engineering'. Professor Morgenthau believes this faith to be an illusion. And further, he believes that our present lack of success in politics springs from a preoccupation with this misleading enterprise. What are his reasons?

He has three main lines of argument, not all equally cogent. The first, and the strongest, is, briefly, that the faith assumes the social world to be 'susceptible to rational control conceived after the model of the natural sciences, while the experiences, domestic and international, of the age contradict this assumption'. That is, rationalistic politics cannot help failing because 'it has misconstrued the nature of politics and political action altogether'.

This argument is, I think, most effective while it remains at what may be called an informal level. Without asserting that human beings are basically and metaphysically selfish, Professor Morgenthau observes (as others have observed before him) that egoism is a characteristic of human behaviour, and that egoism involves a desire for power and the exercise of power over other human beings. The faith he is considering assumes that this egoism is a potentially wasting defect in human nature, the eradication of which is within the competence of scientific knowledge properly applied; but the whole of human experience goes to show that this is, in fact, an illusion. There is no evidence at all that greater knowledge of the causes of human actions itself leads to less egotistical behaviour. On the contrary, such knowledge when it is at the disposal of a supreme egoist merely gives him a greater opportunity of exercising his egoistic intentions more successfully. And further, Professor Morgenthau suggests, the failure of the politics which spring from this faith is due to the manner in which they convert political realities into generalized abstractions – a war to end all wars, in place of a war to defeat a recognizable mischief; a classless society as the solution for all internal discord; national self-determination, a just distribution of raw materials, the four freedoms, the establishment of complete commercial interdependence among nations, or universal socialism, as the ground of universal peace. In short, the failure of this form of politics is the failure that can be forecast for all ideological politics. The purposes pursued and the enterprises embarked upon under the inspiration of this faith are bound, by their abstractness, generality and claim to absolute and permanent validity, to be rigid and consequently to be (or to become in the course of time) out of touch with concrete, specific realities of any political occasion.

But Professor Morgenthau's argument is not concerned with the mere fact of failure. What he proposes to show is not merely that this faith has failed to produce the works claimed to belong to it but to show that this failure is inherent in the faith itself: a science of politics is self-contradictory.

The reader must be left to discover for himself the whole detail of the argument. It is central to the book, and it owes something to both Augustine and Hobbes: since the faith which is being condemned is the modern successor to that of Pelagius, the argument which exposes it is a new anti-Pelagianism. But, briefly, it runs as follows: 'Whatever man does or intends to do emanates from himself and refers again to himself. . . . All action, on the other hand, bears positively and negatively upon others. . . . [But] if the connectedress of the self with others through his action is inevitable, the moral conflict between self and others is no less inevitable.' For, every man has a moral obligation to act unselfishly, an obligation which however, he cannot fulfil without preserving at least that degree of selfishness in his life which is required to maintain himself as an individual capable of performing unselfish acts. 'Once the very logic of the ethics of unselfishness has thus put its stamp of approval on selfishness, individual egoisms, all equally legitimate, confront each other; and the war of every man against every man is on. There are two reasons why the egotism of one must come into conflict with the egotism of the other. What the one wants for himself, the other already possesses or wants too. Struggle and competition ensue. Finding that all his relations with his fellow-men contain at least the germs of such conflicts of interest, man can no longer seek the goodness of his intentions in the almost complete absence of selfishness and of the concomitant harm to others but only in the limitations which conscience puts upon the drive towards evil. Man cannot hope to be good but must be content with being not too evil.

'The other root of conflict and concomitant evil stems from the *animus dominandi*, the desire for power. This lust for power manifests itself as the desire to maintain the range of one's own person with regard to others, to increase it, or to demonstrate it. In whatever disguises it may appear, its ultimate essence and aim is in one of these particular references of one person to others. Centred as it is upon the person of the actor in relation to others, the desire for power is closely related to the selfishness of which we have spoken, but it is not identical with it. For the typical goals of selfishness, such as food, shelter, security, and the means by which they are obtained, such as money, jobs, marriage and the like, have an objective relationship to the vital needs of the individual; their attainment offers the best chances for survival under the particular natural and social conditions under which the individual lives.

'The desire for power, on the other hand, concerns itself not with the individual's survival but with his position among his fellows once his survival has been secured. Consequently, the selfishness of man has limits; his will to power has none. For while a man's vital needs are capable of satisfaction, his lust for power would be satisfied only if the last man became an object of his domination, there being nobody above or beside him, that is, if he became like God.'

This limitless lust for power is the evil spring of all human activity, and consequently of that form of human activity called politics. Politics is merely one of the spheres in which the human *animus dominandi* expresses itself. 'The evil that corrupts political action is the same evil that corrupts all action, but the corruption of political action is indeed the paradigm and the prototype of all possible corruption. The distinction between private and political action is not one between innocence and guilt, morality and immorality, goodness and evil, but lies in the degree alone in which the two types of action deviate from the ethical norm.'

Now, the assumption of rationalism is that the conflict which springs from the human *animus dominandi* can be resolved, and the *animus* itself expelled; and that what is required for the salvation of mankind is nothing more than the exercise of human reason. And the assumption of rationalism in politics is that, by the exercise of human skill (in the form of social engineering), the *animus dominandi* characteristics of politics can, similarly, be resolved, and the *animus* exorcized. But this, if we have followed Professor Morgenthau's argument, is absurd; the *animus* is inherent in the nature of man and human activity and nothing whatever can abolish it. In short, the enterprise of a science of politics rests upon a radical error with regard to the nature of political activity. The human race lacks what would be required to abolish 'power politics'; and all that distinguishes 'scientific man' is his illusion of possessing what is wanting to the human race.

I do not propose to offer any criticism of this argument. Its main principles belong to a tradition of European thought many centuries old; and, if it is no more, it is at least a cogent criticism of the neo-Pelagian assumptions of 'scientism'.

The two other arguments with which Professor Morgenthau supports his view that the prevailing faith in the possibility of a science of politics is illusory, are less well-considered. They are both unconvincing because they rest respectively upon a confusion between scientific enquiry and 'scientism', and between rationality and 'rationalism'. The difficulty of applying the methods of scientific enquiry to human society, the impossibility of properly controlled experiment, the intractability of the material, and the disappointingly slow progress of the enquirers – all this and much like it we have heard before, and the best that can be said of it is that it is wholly irrelevant. And the attempt to discredit a science of society by an appeal to the plausible eccentricities of Eddington's theory of scientific knowledge is equally ill-considered. There is so much to be said in criticism of a science of politics, and Professor Morgenthau has said so much of it, that it is disappointing to find his argument straying in so unprofitable a direction. Sociologists are sensitive to criticism of their methods of en-quiry, but they have, rightly, long ago ceased to be disturbed by this sort of criticism.

And when he turns to show that rationalist politics must fail because man is, in part, irrational, the possessor of 'ir-rational faculties', 'emotional interests and impulses', Professor Morgenthau is guilty of a similar mis-statement of his own position. And it is a dangerous mis-statement, because it makes him appear the opponent of reason, whereas he is only the opponent of rationalism. The idea that human behaviour can-not be reduced to the interaction of the abstractions of ration-alism is confused with the idea that there are areas of human behaviour inherently impervious to rational analysis, and the confusion is fatal to the argument. It is most important that the line of reflection which Professor Morgenthau is pursuing, perhaps the most profitable in political thought at the present time, should not be confused with the mysticism of the higher nonsense, because, in fact, they have nothing in common.

5

To distinguish the character of rationalism in politics and to show that 'the idea of "social engineering", by over-simplifying and distorting the relation between reason and the social world, holds out a hope for a solution of social problems which is bound to be disappointed over and over again', is the main theme of Professor Morgenthau's essay. But he offers, also, some indication of the kind of politics which he would expect to succeed where rationalism fails. And here again his percep-tion is more acute than his argument. In principle, of course, the politics which will succeed will be politics adjusted to human nature and especially to the permanent (but not ex-clusive) egoism of human behaviour. The enterprise of these politics will be to make use of the *strongest*, and not merely the *highest*, human impulses in a continuous attempt to correct ascertainable mischiefs and to suppress actual malpractices in society, but without turning either the mischiefs or their cure into abstract principles, and without being led away by the illusory project of establishing permanent justice in the world. For such a view, politics is the art of the statesman (the art of choosing the least evil of the available courses of action), and is not the rationalism of the social engineer, the supposed science of perfecting human society: the distinction is that which Disraeli indicated when he said, 'My objection to Liberalism is this, that it is the introduction into the practical business of life of the highest kind – namely politics – of philosophical ideas instead of political principles.' Politics is the art of the morally and physically possible; and the practice of this art will, in fact, bring more (and more lasting) benefit to mankind than the pursuit of the enterprise of perfection. But when Professor Morgenthau begins to elaborate an argument to support the general principles of what I should call rational (though not rationalist) politics, he is less convincing. First, he directs our attention to a 'pre-rationalist age' in European history, and to the 'pre-rationalist tradition' of European political thinking. That there is a non-rationalist tradition is, of course, certain, but it did not suddenly come to an end with the appearance of modern rationalism; and the hint of a past golden age of true and successful politics is certainly fanciful. Secondly, he says nothing about the art of statesmanship except that it involves 'a knowledge of a different and a higher order' than that which belongs to the social engineer, and the use of 'higher faculties of mind'. This comes pretty close to the higher nonsense, which we should avoid if we can. What, of course, the states-man requires is nothing higher than the ordinary 'faculties' and ordinary knowledge that everyone (even the convinced rationalist) uses every day in the conduct of his life and in his relations with other men. The vice of the rationalist is not a denial of 'higher faculties', but a misapprehension about the quite ordinary faculties which he and the rest of mankind constantly call upon. And thirdly, Professor Morgenthau suggests that the statesman should be aware of the 'tragic sense of life', of 'the unresolved discord, contradictions and conflicts which are inherent in the nature of things and which human reason is powerless to solve' – a tragic sense which the social scientist lacks. This is all very well; we know what he is trying to say, but it is an unfortunate way of expressing it. Human life is not 'tragic', either in part or as a whole: tragedy belongs to art, not to life. And further, the situation he describes – the imperfectibility of man – is not tragic, nor even a predicament, unless and until it is contrasted with a human nature susceptible of a perfection which is in fact foreign to its character, and rationalism rears its ugly head once more in any argument which assumes or asserts this contrast. To children and to romantic women, but to no one else, it may appear 'tragic' that we cannot enjoy Spring without Winter, eternal youth, and passion always at the height of its beginning. And only a rationalistic reformer will confuse the imperfections which can be remedied with the so-called imperfection which cannot, and will think of the irremovability of the latter as a tragedy. The rest of us know that no rationalistic justice (with its project of approximating people to things), and no possible degree of human prosperity, can ever remove mercy and charity from their place of first importance in the relations of human beings, and know also that this situation cannot properly be considered either imperfect or a tragedy.

6

There remains one more point of importance to be considered. Professor Morgenthau identifies this project of scientific politics with 'liberalism'. And he says that among the institutions by means of which liberalism promoted this enterprise were 'popularly elected parliaments which would subject apparently conflicting views and interests to the test of reason through intelligent discussion'. But he observes also that the pundits of a science of politics have never been able to find more than a secondary place (perhaps no place at all) for parliamentary institutions. And he quotes Lester Ward, one of the apostles of sociology, as follows:

> Legislative bodies will doubtless need to be maintained, and every new law should be finally adopted by a vote of such bodies, but more and more this will become a merely formal way of putting the final sanction of society on decisions that have been carefully worked out in what may be called the sociological laboratory. Legislation will consist in a series of exhaustive experiments on the part of true scientific sociologists and sociological inventors working on problems of social physics from the practical point of view. It will undertake to solve not only questions of general

interest to the State . . . but questions of social improvement, the amelioration of the condition of all the people, the removal of whatever privations may still remain, and the adoption of means to the positive increase of the social welfare, in short the organization of human happiness.

Now, there is little evidence that Professor Morgenthau has given any thought to these apparently opposed elements in the enterprise of a science of politics, which is both surprising and disappointing: surprising, because it is on his own reading of history that the opposition appears to be within liberalism itself; disappointing, because if he had reflected upon it he might have seen the true state of affairs, which is, that parliamentary government and rationalist politics do not belong to the same tradition and do not, in fact, go together. Professor Morgenthau, in common with many Americans and almost all continental writers, believes erroneously that parliamentary institutions were the offspring of rationalist politics. This is, perhaps, an excusable error, because in America and on the continent of Europe parliamentary institutions were in fact coeval with the full flood of rationalistic politics, and because the proper antidote to this error is a knowledge of the only history that matters in this connection, the history of England. But the same illusion is entertained, less excusably, by Englishmen when they speak of 'democratic planning'; rationalist planning may, they think, be 'democratic' because they believe (not from the history and experience of their own society but on the word of a set of ignorant foreigners) that 'democracy' and scientific politics sprang from the same root. The truth is, however, that the institutions of parliamentary government sprang from the least rationalistic period of our politics, from the Middle Ages, and (despite the cloud of false theory with which recent centuries have enveloped them) were connected, not with the promotion of a rationalist order of society, but (in conjunction with the common law) with the limitation of the exercise of political power and the opposition to tyranny in whatever from it appeared. The root of so-called 'democratic' theory is not rationalist optimism about the perfectibility of human society, but scepticism about the possibility of such perfection and the determination not to allow human life to be perverted by the tyranny of a person or fixed by the tyranny of an idea. And the failure to detect and to elucidate the radical opposition of parliamentary institutions and the values they represent to rationalist politics is one more piece of evidence of the danger of a system of education in which boys and girls grind out their little lessons in civics (as they used, more profitably, to grind out their Latin grammar) instead of acquiring, from the actual history of their society, some insight into their own political tradition.

8

THE CUSTOMER
IS NEVER WRONG

1955

For many years now Mr Walter Lippmann,[1] a distinguished
American writer, has been one of the most thoughtful observers
of the way the world seems to have been going; and in several
books he has reflected upon the general march of events and
upon many of its incidents. My business now is to comment on
his latest work. But, first, I ought to say what it is about and to
describe its thesis.

A Book about Contemporary Politics

The Public Philosophy[2] is a book about contemporary politics;
and, in particular, it is about the vices and virtues of what we
call – understanding among ourselves near enough what we
mean – 'liberal democracy'. This is not a new theme, particularly with American writers, who in this matter sometimes
display the defensiveness of an anxious parent. But if there is

[1] Walter Lippmann was born in New York City in 1889 and died there in 1974.
During a sixty-year career, he became one of the world's foremost newspaper
columnists and political commentators. At Harvard he studied under William
James and George Santayana. He helped found *The New Republic* in 1914. He
influenced Woodrow Wilson's concept of a post-war peace settlement, and partici-
pated in the negotiations at Versailles. He authored many remarkable books,
including *Public Opinion* (1922) and *The Good Society* (1937). *Essays in the Public
Philosophy* appeared in 1955 to some acclaim among the 'new conservatives' of post-
World War II America. American liberals criticized it for its defence of natural law.
Oakeshott's critique differs from each of these: his is an application of his outlook as
a political philosopher, elaborated in other essays in the present volume. (*Timothy
Fuller*)
[2] Hamish Hamilton, 12s. 6d.

any tinge of parental concern in Mr Lippmann's writing, it appears in the severity of his judgement and not in a disposition to excuse shameful conduct.

In his opinion, liberal democratic government during this century has been tried and found wanting in two important respects: it has revealed itself as an unsuccessful manner of conducting public affairs, and it has allowed its structure of beliefs to become dilapidated. The neglect of these beliefs is taken to be the cause of the practical failure. The liberal democrat finds himself, first, demoralized by being unable to defend his beliefs cogently, and then intimidated by his practical failure and by the confidence of his opponents. In short, liberal democracy is on the run: the typical revolutions of recent times are those in which this manner of conducting affairs has been destroyed; and where it has survived, it is manifestly diseased. The symptom that attracts Mr Lippmann's attention is the failure of liberal-democratic governments both in war and in peace. In war they have managed to avoid defeat, but only by calling for immense sacrifices from their subjects, the price of which has been the corruption of public policy by the delusions of public opinion. And, for the same reason, after two wars, these governments have failed 'to bring peace and order to the world'.

The disease of liberal-democratic government, then, is diagnosed as 'a functional derangement of the relationship between the mass of the people and the government'. The masses have acquired power; but it turns out to be merely the power to inhibit the rational conduct of policy. They are averse from change, intolerant of compromise, unaware of danger until disaster appears, and every situation is simplified to distortion in their minds. And since the tenure of a government now depends upon their approval, governing has ceased to be an activity of making rational decisions about current situations. In short, the partners in the conduct of affairs (a governing authority, an elected assembly and the electors), each of whom has a proper office to perform, have become disarranged: the electorate has usurped the place of the government.

Intellectual Derangement

What treatment does Mr Lippmann prescribe? As he understands it, the derangement, at bottom, is intellectual. This incorrect disposition of the partners is the product of a 'philosophy' which sanctifies even the most wanton desires of the masses: the philosophy of Jacobinism. Consequently, in looking for a cure, Mr Lippmann turns to expound another philosophy (calling it 'the public philosophy') which he believes to be the foundation of the proper order of the partners in a healthy and effective liberal-democratic manner of government.

This 'public philosophy' is not offered as an invention of his own. He believes that there is still to hand the philosophy of the founders of this manner of conducting affairs, and that the renewal of democratic order and vitality may be expected to spring from a revival of this neglected philosophy. To those familiar with the history of European thought on this matter, it will be enough to say that Mr Lippmann's 'public philosophy' is a doctrine of natural law – the belief (to put it in the form he favours) that there are absolute principles in the conduct of affairs which all men, when they are sincerely and lucidly rational, will agree to be self-evidently true; and the belief that these principles are the terms of the good life for human beings in this world. If these beliefs were once more to become 'the public philosophy', they would give back to liberal-democratic society the sense of a rational public interest to be pursued, and liberal-democratic governments would be released from their present servitude to the desires and opinions of the masses.

This vigorously argued thesis raises difficult points at each step. It has the virtue of calling attention to what is important, and it is refreshingly free from the claptrap about 'capitalism' that has for so long disfigured political discussion. But in the end I do not find it very convincing.

Misplaced Gloom?

First, Mr Lippmann takes a gloomy view of the prospects of liberal-democratic government; but his gloom appears to me both exaggerated and misplaced. It is clear that he has had hopes which have been disappointed; but they were not very reasonable hopes. It is not to be expected that any manner of conducting affairs will be an unqualified success; and to expect this of the liberal-democratic manner (which depends pre-eminently upon hardly acquired habits of moderation) is to expect altogether too much. To grumble, or even to be disheartened, because it has not brought definitive peace and order to the world is to judge it by an inappropriate standard. Moreover, is it not a trifle hasty to construe what has happened in Russia, in Italy, Germany, Spain, Portugal, and Argentina as examples of a recession from liberal-democratic government? In which of these places was this manner of conducting affairs ever properly understood or firmly established? The fact is that, although its incautious friends have taught us to regard this manner of government as the inevitable good fortune in store for all mankind, its practice has so far been confined to a very small part of the world. There has been little genuine recession; and the conditions of even moderate success are so severe that we ought not to be surprised if there has, also, been little genuine extension.

But, if the disappointment of unreasonable hopes should lose us no sleep, and if the notion of great areas of the world recently lost to liberal democracy is an illusion, the difficulties that have appeared in this manner of government are real enough. And while Mr Lippmann's account of them seems to me acute and fair, I question it in one respect.

It was long ago observed that where large masses of men participate in it, the activity of governing becomes infected with formulas and crude generalizations, with unreasoning affections and indelible hatreds; if reflection exists, it is swamped by powerful and irrelevant personal memories; and incantation readily takes the place of reasoning. And the result is that the activity of governing is rarely in touch with the current situation. And when Mr Lippmann detects immobility and abstraction as the propensities of popular political opinion, no doubt he is right. But his contention that these abstractions and generalities, these compulsive loves and hates and desires, are somehow spontaneously generated in 'the people', and that the politician finds himself in the unfortunate position of having them imposed upon him, seems to me false. The formulas which are the idiom of popular political opinion, even the popular memories which divert attention from current situations, are not imposed upon politicians; they are invented, provoked, and excited by politicians (and, it is fair to say, journalists) in search of power. It is safe to say that we, 'the people', never ask for what we have not been prompted to desire; we corrupt policy, not by our own shortsighted demands, but by our responsiveness to what is suggested and promised to us. Our voice is loud, but our utterance is the repetition of simple lessons well learned. Our only distinction as participants in liberal-democratic government is that we have a variety of teachers and that we do not all repeat the same lesson. In short, there is no doubt that the liberal-democratic manner of conducting affairs is prone to a certain sort of corruption, but I think Mr Lippmann's account of it is not quite convincing.

As Mr Lippmann sees it, the only sure defence against this corruption is the revival and common acceptance of a certain set of beliefs about government. But, from what he has already said about the propensities of popular political opinion, I should have expected him to write off this revival as desirable but impossible. Where is the *point d'appui* in popular opinion for his understanding of politics as an activity governed by self-evidently rational principles? Indeed, where are the principles themselves? Moreover, the Jacobin philosophy is so exactly adapted to popular understanding that I can see no reason why he should permit himself the hope that it might be superseded in that quarter by this philosophy of natural law. And it is at this point that I find myself taking a somewhat less gloomy view than Mr Lippmann. For I believe that the functional derangement of the partners in liberal-democratic government is held in check, not by the relics of a philosophy of natural law in popular opinion, but, if not on all occasions by the relics of courage and integrity among politicians, then by their share in common human vices. The propensity of all modern leaders (politicians included) is to become demagogues; and what holds a man back from being a demagogue is not a complicated intellectual doctrine about the nature of government, but some simple moral qualities: courage, or perhaps pride, or indifference, or even mere laziness.

Freedom of Speech

But, be that how it may, a theory of what politics is about is not wholly irrelevant in this connection, and it is worth while to consider what Mr Lippmann has to say of it. After some discussion of the general contents of his public philosophy he gives examples of its teaching in respect of two liberal-democratic institutions: property and freedom of speech. I think he is mistaken in what he says about both, but I will confine myself to the second. The large manner in which liberal democrats have talked about freedom of speech has got them into trouble: this is the door through which Jacobin tyranny has entered. But, says Mr Lippmann, freedom of speech properly understood would offer no entrance for Jacobinism. And properly understood it belongs to the corpus of liberal-democratic rights only when it is recognized as 'a method of attaining moral and political truth'. Its counterpart is the obligation to be a *bona fide* participant in a debate whose object is to elicit 'truth'. To absolve oneself from this obligation is to surrender the right of freedom of speech.

This seems to me a great error. And so far from hindering the appearance of the heresy of Jacobinism, it is itself a Jacobin theory. For wherever, in modern times, free speech has been suppressed, it has always been because 'truth' is believed to have been attained, and what is suppressed is recognised as mere error. 'Truth' seekers in politics are potential enemies of free speech because they are unprotected against the belief that they have reached their goal. And what makes popular opinion a corrupting influence upon the conduct of government is precisely its readiness to believe that the current formulas represent 'the truth'.

But why in fact do we cherish the right to speak freely? Because we have become a people with a variety of opinions about all sorts of matters and we do not see why we should not utter them. We know that there are limits to this right, but we know also that these limits have nothing whatever to do with 'truth' and 'error', but only with peace and tranquillity. The proper rationale of free speech, and the limits commonly imposed upon it by liberal-democratic governments, is not the belief that every utterance is a *bona fide* participation in a search for some one 'truth', but the belief that politics are not concerned with this sort of 'truth' at all. They are concerned with the cultivation of what from time to time are accepted as the peaceable decencies of conduct among men who do not suffer from the Puritan-Jacobin illusion that in practical affairs there is an attainable condition of things called 'truth' or 'perfection'. Jacobinism is politics in which 'truth' as opposed to 'error' is sought, and consequently in which speech is recognized as argument and is permitted, but only until 'truth' appears. Liberal democracy is, on the other hand, sceptical politics, in which 'truth' appears not as the opposite of 'error' but merely as the opposite of 'lies', and in which utterance is largely free because it is recognized not as argument but conversation. If we want instruction about the theory of liberal-democratic freedom of speech it is not to Milton or to Mill that we should go, but to Montaigne and Hume.

There is one other feature of Mr Lippmann's argument that should be noticed. 'The free political institutions of the western world', he writes, 'were conceived and established by men who believed that honest reflection on the common experience of mankind would always cause men to come to the same ultimate conclusion. Within the Golden Rule of the same philosophy for elucidating their ultimate end, they could engage with confident hope in the progressive discovery of truth'. This raises the question of the relationship between a manner of conducting public affairs (such as the liberal-democratic manner) and a set of abstract beliefs. That there is a relationship of some sort, nobody can doubt: all modern political activity has as its counterpart doctrines of some kind. Mr Lippmann's view is that every manner conducting affairs has a doctrine as its 'foundation' or 'premiss' or 'cause'. Belief in a doctrine of government generates a manner of governing. And, consequently, he understands correct doctrine to be of the first importance.

Nobody would deny that it is important to have our general ideas about government as straight as we can get them; but the notion that practice derives from theory in this simple manner is, I think, a mistake. When Mr Lippmann says that the founders of our free institutions were adherents of the philosophy of natural law, and that 'the free political institutions of the Western world were conceived and established' by men who held certain abstract beliefs, he speaks with the shortened perspective of an American way of thinking in which a manner of conducting affairs is inconceivable without an architect and without a premeditated 'dedication to a proposition'. But the fact is that nobody ever 'founded' these institutions. They are the product of innumerable human choices, over long stretches of time, but not of any human design. And the choices from which they sprang were not responses to abstract beliefs, but to current situations. It is illuminating to be told that the characters of Shakespeare 'represent' in their actions and utterances some theory of human conduct – Aristotle's or Seneca's; and it is illuminating to have revealed to us the doctrine of government which partners a manner of governing. But the notion that our manner of governing was invented according to a doctrine and without this doctrine would be without vitality, is as false as the notion that Dogberry, or even Hamlet, was generated from a formula without which his conduct would be meaningless. General political ideas are not the 'cause' or the 'foundation' of conduct; they are conduct itself in another idiom. That is why it is so often possible for Mr Lippmann to be acute in his observation of the virtues and vices of the liberal-democratic manner of conducting affairs, but to be as often misled in his exploration of the theory which is its intellectual counterpart.

Somebody once said that whenever a new book was published he always read an old one. If on this occasion you find yourself that way inclined I do not think you could do better than to turn from *Public Philosophy* to Sir Henry Maine's book, *Popular Government*, published seventy years ago.

9

THE CONCEPT OF
A PHILOSOPHY OF POLITICS

1946(?)

I

Lately I have had occasion to consider the writings of Hobbes. (And, in common with others, I found it not difficult to determine the relation for example, of his *Leviathan* to its time. This book has often and successfully been regarded as a tract for the times. But the attempts which have been made to show that it is nothing other and nothing more than this have, I think, been less successful.) And in reading the *Leviathan* I seem to find, not only a book the significance of which lies in the seventeenth century, not only a book which offers an explanation of the origin and character of political life constructed to meet particular circumstances, but to find also something which, because it can relevantly be separated from time and place and for other reasons, I should call a philosophy of politics. And of course this has been observed before. But the question arose: by what standard or criticism should the success or failure of such a philosophy of politics be determined? The success or failure of a tract for the times is easy enough to determine. And, if it is not easy to determine it, we at least know how to determine the success or failure of a political theory which confines itself to the presentation of a view of what is ideal or what ought to be. We know pretty clearly what, in general, to expect from these and other kinds of political writings. But in order to determine the success or failure of a philosophy of politics we require a view of what we may expect from such a philosophy as distinct from what we may expect from other kinds of political thought; and that to me at least, is not so clear. I do not mean that we must know in advance the results which we should expect a philosophy of politics to achieve; I mean that we must have some general view of the *kind* of results we expect from it. What we require is a fully defined concept of a philosophy of politics.

2

Now, the ideas on this subject which I found in my head were, I think, the usual ideas. And I found them pretty vague, unconvincing and unsatisfactory. They centered round a view of the character of philosophy which appeared to be erroneous; and they failed to give a coherent account of the character of a philosophy of politics. But I think it will be useful to consider them for a moment.

A philosophy of politics, it appears, is a general view or explanation of the nature of social and political life and activity from the standpoint of its purpose and end. A philosophy of politics is concerned with that part of human life and those particular actions which involve and are involved in the existence of society. Occasionally a philosophy of politics is to be found more narrowly conceived as a general explanation of the character of *political* life and activity from the standpoint of its purpose and, as distinct from merely *social* life and activity. And where this is so, a philosophy of politics becomes a general view of the nature of the state from the standpoint of its purpose and end.

But this broad conception has been made more precise. A philosophy of politics, conceived first in this way, has become the analysis and relation of a certain small number of general concepts. The concepts in question may be divided into three groups, though I do not propose this as anything like an exhaustive enumeration of them.

(i) Self, society, law, government, the state.

(ii) Right and wrong, good and bad, ought and ought not (obligation and duty).

(iii) Political obligation, sovereignty, liberty, equality, justice and punishment.

These concepts are taken to give a general outline of political life and activity, they are a kind of first discrimination of this character of political life, and it is with these that a philosophy of politics is concerned.

So far, I think, we have a fairly precise notion of what is meant by a philosophy of politics. But, of course, it requires a good deal of amplification before anything which could be called a fully defined concept of a philosophy of politics appears. We require to know exactly what a philosophy of politics is to do with these concepts, to know what is meant by 'analysis and relation'. And I think that what is vague, unsatisfactory and unconvincing is the usual account we are given of what a philosophy of politics is to do with these concepts. And if this is so, I take it to imply that, in spite of the *prima facie* precision of this concept of a philosophy of politics, it is really only half-thought-out and as it stands incoherent. In particular there are three aspects of this concept to which I want to call attention.

1. This concept of a philosophy of politics, notwithstanding what may be actively asserted, implies that a philosophy of politics is, somehow, not itself genuinely philosophical. A philosophy of politics is conceived as the application of certain previously thought-out philosophical ideas, or of some previously thought-out general philosophical doctrine, to political life and activity. Thus, we have a philosophy of politics built upon general philosophical ideas derived from Bergson, and another built upon the philosophical theory which goes by the name of pragmatism, and a third built upon a form of idealistic philosophy. The business of a philosophy of politics is to conceive political life and activity in such a way as to make them appear to *illustrate* some such philosophical doctrine as these. The philosophy of politics is itself nothing more than a special instance, a special application of a general philosophical theory; it merely exemplifies or illustrates. And the analysis of concepts consists in presenting these concepts within the lines of some established or appropriated philosophical doctrine.

Now, if this be the case, it follows that the genuinely philosophical part of a philosophy of politics is something prior to and independent of the analysis of political concepts which the philosophy of politics itself comprises. Philosophy is related to a philosophy of politics merely as a presupposition. And this analysis of political concepts, which is taken to be the actual business of a philosophy of politics, is not itself a philosophical analysis, it is merely an analysis which presupposes some philosophical outline or other. But it is perhaps worth remark that in many of these philosophies of politics, what is conceived as the 'philosopy' and is distinguished as prior to the actual analysis of political ideas, is taken over ready-made, and is commonly appropriated for some entirely non-philosophical reason – because it 'appeals' to the prejudices or the temperament of the political thinker. Philosophies of politics conceived in this way are rarely the work of philosophical thinkers. And this, I think, is what we should expect.

According to this concept of a philosophy of politics, then, such a philosophy is philosophical only in the sense that it is an analysis of political ideas presented as an example of some general philosophical doctrine. And, as a rule, the general philosophical doctrine of which a philosophy of politics is taken to be illustrative is supposed to consist, in the first place, of some ethical doctrine, and secondly of some metaphysical doctrine. A philosophy of politics is an illustration of a special application of an ethical and a metaphysical theory. Often the ethical doctrine is thought of as itself based upon, as itself illustrative of, the metaphysical doctrine. And where this is the case, the philosophy of politics is, apparently, at two removes from genuinely philosophical thought, it is an illustration of an illustration of a philosophical theory.

This concept of a philosophy of politics implies, then, that a philosophy of politics is philosophical in only a derivative sense. It is philosophical merely because it is, somehow, based upon a philosophy. And a philosophy of politics, that is, an analysis of political concepts, which itself became genuinely philosophical would at once defeat its own end. It would return into the general philosophical theory from which it was, in fact, derived, and cease to have any evident connection with political life and activity.

2. The second aspect which I wish to discuss of this concept of a philosophy of politics presents this fundamentally semi-philosophical and anomalous character of a philosophy of politics more definitely. When we turn to consider the general criticism of truth which this concept takes to govern a philosophy of politics, we find once more, I think, that a philosophy of politics is here implicitly defined as something which is not itself philosophical.

It is, of course, at least formally admitted that a philosophy of politics must be a reasoned and coherent body of concepts; unless it were that it could not pretend to be a philosophy in any sense. A philosophy of politics must be a rationalization of political life and activity. But it has, besides, another master; it has to conform to the so-called 'facts of political life'. And by the 'facts of political life' is meant the character of political life as it is conceived by the ordinary, commonsense observer, the observer whose mind is yet uncloaked by philosophical speculation. But further, since to the ordinary observer political life is, perhaps the aspect of life least subject to the rule of reason, the two allegiances which a philosophy of politics is required to admit may be expected frequently to conflict. And in the event of such a conflict, there is no doubt about which criticism a philosophy of politics is called upon to accept and which reject. It must, at all costs, conform to the 'facts of political life'. And, things being what they are, a rationalized account of political activity may be expected to misrepresent its character, may be expected to be false to the 'facts of political life'. A philosophy of politics, therefore, is likely to be unsound if it partakes too fully of a philosophical character. And this dilemma, this anomalous character, is not peculiar to some particular philosophies of politics; it is common to all philosophies of politics constructed in agreement with this concept of a philosophy of politics, that is, it is common to a very large number of hitherto constructed philosophies of politics.

A few examples by way of illustration:

(a) It is said, with some truth, that to the ordinary observer one of the most undesirable features of social and political life is the great variety of purposes and ends for which men act. And it is asserted that a philosophy of politics which does not accept this variety as a fixed and unalterable *datum* must be unsound. There are, of course, many ways in which it may be accepted; but in one way or another it must be accepted unconditionally. And yet, more unconditioned variety is exactly what reason rejects; it is what a philosophy of politics, if its aim were to give a purely rational account of political life, must find some way of superseding. A philosophy of politics, therefore, it appears, is perpetually faced with the choice of being rational or being 'true' – true to the 'facts of political life'.

(b) Or consider the grounds upon which the philosophical concept of a 'general will' is rejected and defended: for, I think, many of its defenders are as much at fault in this respect as many of those who reject it. We look round the world of political activity and disguise the concept of a 'general will' because, we say, a general will is not a phenomenon to be found there. Or we assert and defend this concept on the grounds that, conceived in a certain way, such a phenomenon can be seen to exist. But the rejecters are like Laplace who swept the heavens with his telescope and declared that he could not see God anywhere; and these defenders are like Kant, who, performing the same action, reached the opposite conclusion. Both are attempting to judge a philosophical concept by referring it to the 'facts of political life'.

(c) Or, once more, consider the grounds upon which the concept of 'self-realization' is rejected. We do not find, it is said, men always and everywhere acting with the express purpose of seeking the greatest possible degree of self-realization; we do not find this end constantly present in the minds of legislators and administrators; therefore the concept of self-realization must be rejected – it is a false account of the end sought in political activity.

A philosophy of politics, then, is, according to the concept I am considering, subject to two masters: reason and the 'facts of political life'. But, what is even more serious, there is a third master also competing for recognition. For not only must a philosophy of politics present a thoroughly rationalized account of political life and at the same time conform to the 'facts of political life', but it must also abstain from any view or doctrine which would tend to inhibit or paralyse political activity. A philosophy of politics which, for example, diverted our attention away from the so-called 'fact' that human ends are achieved by human effort, must, for that reason, be unsound. And here, again, the anomalous and semi-philosophical character of a philosophy of politics comes to the surface; for, as I understand it, the inevitable tendency of a philosophy is to inhibit action, and of a genuine philosophy of politics, to inhibit political action.

3. The third aspect of a philosophy of politics conceived in this way which I want to consider is that concerned with the purpose attributed to it. We have seen that a philosophy of politics is expected to give a view of the end in political activity; but when we look closer we discover that what this concept actually expects from a philosophy of politics is the *determination* of the end in political activity. That is, a philosophy of politics is expected to say what that end *should* or *ought to* be. Questions of fact are separated from questions of right, and a philosophy of politics is taken to be concerned, at least ultimately, with questions of right. The business of a philosophy of politics is to find a basis of right, as distinct from

a basis of fact, for human association and the institutions of a politically organized community. In Rousseau's phrase, his subject of a philosophy of politics is 'men as they are and laws as they might be'.

Now, in the view of many people this characteristic will not, perhaps, brand a philosophy of politics as especially non-philosophical. But in my view it does so. The notion that it is the business of a philosophy of any worth actually to determine ends is, I think, false. A philosophy of politics may plausibly be supposed to undertake the task of representing political life as activity in pursuit of some end, and the task of analysing the general concept of an end; but this is quite different from the actual determination of which among many presented ends political activity might choose. And if a genuine philosophy of politics rejects, for example, happiness as the end in political activity, and substitutes 'self-realization', what it is asserting is *not* that happiness and self-realization are two possible ends in political activity and that self-realization ought to be preferred, but that happiness is a false analysis of the end actually sought and that self-realization is a true analysis. That is to say, the judgement implicit and explicit in a genuine philosophy of politics is not a moral judgement about which of many ends is preferable, but a purely logical judgement about which of many analyses is true. And yet, it appears, what is expected for a philosophy of politics is a moral judgement of this kind. A philosophical theory does not, in practice, arise from dis-content with the present organization of society, or dislike of the ends which a particular society seems to be setting for itself; and it cannot be supposed to be designed to satisfy such a discontent. To expect this from it is, I think, to expect something which it could never give. And whatever does satisfy a discontent of this sort, is, for that reason not a genuinely philosophical theory.

3

So far I have been considering the ideas which I found in my head when I sat down to consider what should be expected from a philosophy of politics. And the general concept of a philosophy of politics which they appeared to imply seems to me, as I have remarked, extremely incoherent and un-convincing. A philosophy of politics, according to this view, is really nothing better than a contradiction. It is a philosophy which, for more than one reason, is not philosophical, and one which, if it became genuinely philosophical would cease to have anything to do with politics. At best it seems to be a mere illustration of a philosophical doctrine to which it contributes nothing. It is said to be built upon a philosophy, but when it is examined there appears to be nothing at all philosophical about the superstructure itself. It is said to imply a philosophy; but the philosophical doctrine is never taken to imply the political theory, expect in the doubtful sense in which a general view may be said to imply a special instance. It recognizes, moreover, a criticism which is anything but philosophical – that of conformity to the so-called 'facts of political life'; and it claims a purpose which at once distinguishes it from anything which could be called philosophical – that of telling us what, either in general or in detail, we ought to aim at in political activity.

Now, I take it that there is something wrong with a concept which presents it subject as essentially anomalous and self-contradictory. I take it that there is something wrong with a concept which asserts, almost explicitly, that a philosophy of politics is not philosophical. We are left with the alternative, either of accepting this as the best we can do and confessing that there is, and can be, no such thing as a philosophy of politics in any intelligible sense of the phrase, or of thinking out a less vague and more coherent concept of a philosophy of politics. I propose, for the sake of argument, to take the second, and make an attempt to present a concept of a philosophy of politics less incoherent than the one I seem to have inherited. To encourage one there is the suggestion that at least two distinguished writers have produced philosophies of political life which imply quite a different concept of a philosophy of politics than that which I have been discussing – I mean, Hobbes and Hegel.

4

A philosophy of politics I should describe in general terms, as – *an explanation or view of political life and activity from the standpoint of the totality of experience*. It is the attempt, not to *separate* political life and activity from everything else in human experience and to treat them as if they were *sui generis* and belonged to a world of their own; but, in the first place, to *distinguish* political life and activity within the totality of experience; and secondly, to *relate* them to the totality so that they are seen in their place in the totality.

A philosophy of politics conceived in this way may, like that conceived in the other way, be reduced to the analysis of a small number of general concepts. But in this case the analysis will be of quite a different character from that suggested in the other concept of a philosophy of politics; it will itself be a philosophical analysis and not merely an analysis based upon some presupposed philosophical doctrine. I prefer not to call it an 'analysis' at all for the word is, I think, misleading: in these days it has almost become a technical term and the private property of a single school of philosophies. The business of a philosophy of politics is, rather, the complete, or philosophical, *definition* of these concepts.

Now, in order to make this concept of a philosophy of politics clear, I must define in slightly greater detail the concept of philosophy which it implies, and must indicate, or at least illustrate, the character of the philosophy of politics that would result. But one thing, I think, is clear already: the fatal weakness of the concept of a philosophy of politics which I have previously discussed is not merely that it denies a genuinely philosophical character to a philosophy of politics, but also that it misconceives the character of philosophy itself when it supposes that a philosophical doctrine, composed of a body of ethical and metaphysical concepts, can be taken over and 'applied' to political life and activity. There is a *confused* concept of a philosophy of politics based upon a *false* concept of philosophy.

Philosophical thought, as I understand it, is not a kind of thought entirely different from all other, and philosophical knowledge is not a special kind of knowledge derived from some special source of information. Philosophical thought and knowledge is simply thought and knowledge *without reservation or presupposition*. The aim in philosophy is to arrive at concepts which, because they presuppose nothing, are complete in themselves; the aim is to define and establish concepts so fully and completely that nothing further remains to be added. Definition is a matter of degree. All thinking is the attempt to define concepts, and philosophy is merely what occurs when thought is allowed to follow its own bent with unqualified freedom. Thought, the character of which is exemplified in

every attempt at intellectual comprehension, is perfectly exemplified in philosophical comprehension. A philosophical
doctrine, therefore, should not be understood as a kind of solid
basis upon which things like science and the conduct of practical life ultimately rest; science and practical life, as such, have
no philosophical foundations. It should be thought of as something which happens at the end, when the concepts of science
or of practical life are subjected to the revolutionary and
dissolving criticism of being related to the totality of experience.
Thus, any incomplete following of the demands of thought has
a constant tendency to *overbalance* into philosophical thought;
for until it has become philosophical it must remain unstable.

The starting place in philosophy, then, is not in some remote
region of experience known only to the philosopher. Philosophy
begins with the concepts of ordinary, everyday knowledge, and
consists in an extended, detailed and complete exposition of
those concepts, an exposition which is itself a definition. In
philosophy, therefore, there is no such thing as a transition
from mere ignorance to complete knowledge; the process is
always one of coming to know more fully what is in some sense
already known. Nor is there such a thing as a mere addition to
knowledge; the process is not always one of radical reformulation of the whole of what is already known. It is not
merely the extension and elaboration of the meaning of a
concept, but the establishment of a new and comprehensive
meaning. The philosophical concept at once comprehends and
supersedes the concept given to philosophical thought.

The process of philosophical definition may be regarded,
from one point of view, as a process of getting rid of, or of
resolving, the presuppositions and reservations contained in
whatever concepts are presented for examination. This is sometimes thought of as a process of laying, or discovering, *foundations*; but it is, I think, misleading to think of it in this way.
For when these presuppositions have been revealed and *a
fortiori*, when they have been resolved, the originally presented
concept has been entirely transformed and superseded. And
moreover, the aim in philosophical definition is not to achieve
concepts with no unexamined or unjustified presuppositions,
but to achieve concrete concepts from which the division between presupposition and conclusion has vanished. Presuppositions and conclusions are alike abstractions and to be got rid
of; and the only way to get rid of them is by establishing
concepts in which the two elements are, not equally well-

known, not merely held together in agreement, but actually unified. The philosophic concept is not a mere union of abstracts, it is not, for example, a scientific concept plus the presuppositions which lie behind it, but is itself a concrete unity. And it is this because it is what a fully defined concept must be.

This, then, is the starting-point, and this is the process; I must say a word about this conclusion. There are four characteristics or attributes of the philosophical concept to which I wish to draw attention. It is (i) New, (ii) Categorical, (iii) Affirmative, (iv) Indicative.

(i) *New.* A philosophical concept is, essentially, the redefinition of an already formulated concept. Philosophy is the attempt to redefine its given concepts concretely, that is in relation to the totality of experience. And consequently a philosophical concept *must* be different from the given concept from which it starts. There *must* be disagreement between a concept as it is for, say, commonsense, and as it is for philosophy. Now, this for many people is a stumbling-block; for them it is proof, or at least a symptom, of the falsehood inseparable from philosophy. But the principle involved seems to be clear and simple. If what is undertaken is a transformation, you must not reject the result if it is different from what you started with. And, of course, this important implication of this principle is that 'verification' in philosophy cannot be by mere 'reference to the facts'. 'The facts' are merely 'our ordinary way of regarding the facts' or 'the concept as it is for commonsense', and those must necessarily be irrelevant to philosophy. It is *Ex hypothesi* impossible for the philosophical concept of, say, justice, to agree with this commonsense concept, and consequently it must be false to suppose that agreement with the commonsense concept is the criteria of which the philosophical concept is to be judged. And moreover, insofar as the philosophical concept is really more complete and more coherent, it must be taken to be superior to the commonsense concept. And to suggest agreement with what is inferior as a test for what is superior is obviously absurd. Nevertheless, although it is an error to suppose that a philosophical definition can be verified by referring it to the so-called 'facts', it is incumbent upon the philosopher to show as fully as he can how his redefinition is connected with and arises from the less comprehensive definition with which he began. That is, his definition must be presented as a conclusion from an exhibited process of inference. A philosopher can establish his definition only by showing in detail the process of definition, and by showing his conclusion to be itself comprehensive. This, of course, is the philosophical method and aim presented to us in the Socratic dialogues; and it is one with which I see no reason to quarrel.

(ii) *Categorical.* A philosophical concept must always be in the form of a categorical judgement. By this, I do not, of course, mean that it may not be tentative; I mean that it may not be hypothetical. Hypotheses are reservations, pre-suppositions; and it is the business of philosophy to get rid of all reservations and presuppositions. But to say that a philosophical concept must be categorical means more than this; it means that definition in philosophy comprehends the whole character of its subject and comprehends it as a single whole. Of course, it is not possible or desirable that every aspect of a concept should be indicated explicitly in a philosophical definition; but if the definition is to be philosophically satisfactory it must be possible to show how it has implicitly included and superseded all other views. A philosophical concept is categorical because it is complete.

(iii) *Affirmative or Positive.* A philosophical concept must always be an affirmative or positive concept, never merely a negative concept. And where the given concept is negative, one part at least of the business of a philosophy is to transform this negative into a positive. This perhaps is only another way of saying that a philosophical concept must be categorical; hypotheses are always a negative element. A merely negative concept, as I understand it, is necessarily incompletely defined; negativity is a common form of incompleteness which philosophy exists to overcome, it is an example of lack of perseverance in thought. For a negative always and unavoidably implies a positive, and until this positive is brought to the surface what we have must remain only partly coherent. For example, any philosophy of politics conceived in terms of the limits of state actions, or any theory of punishment which leaves punishment as merely the exclusion of the criminal from the enjoyment of rights, must be taken to fail philosophically because it fails to transform this negative to a positive. What philosophy is inimical to is compromise, concepts defined in the form of a little of this and a little of that, for compromise is always the sign of lack of completeness in definition, the sign of makeshift.

(iv) *Indicative.* This again is not a separate characteristic, but one implied in the affirmative and categorical character of philosophical concepts. And it means that whenever an imperative is presented, philosophy must transform it into an indicative; wherever 'ought' presents itself the business of philosophy is to uncover the implied 'is'. And again, it is a failure to do this which ruins, philosophically, a great many 'philosophies of politics'. A mere imperative is an abstraction; nothing when related to the totality of experience is merely imperative, and so nothing in philosophy must be left in this mood.

A philosophy of politics, then, as I see it, is not the application to political life of a previously thought out philosophical doctrine, it is not the attempt to illustrate a philosophy by a particular example or instance; it is the attempt to think out to the end the body of concepts which together seem to comprise the world of political activity; it is the attempt to define those political concepts by relating them to the totality of experience. It is not a part of philosophy; but the impulse of philosophic thought making itself manifest in connection with a particular body of concepts.

I want, now, to give an example of the way in which a philosophy of politics should (as I see it) approach these concepts which together seem to comprise the world of political activity. But what I have to say will be very tentative, because I do not pretend to have thought out a complete philosophy of politics for myself. These concepts must not, of course, be regarded as fixed and irreducible; they are merely what a commonsense analysis of political life presents to philosophy, and many of them, in the process of philosophical definition, may disappear altogether. What are presented as two distinct concepts may turn out to be merely two aspects of a single concept, or one may turn out to be merely an aspect of the other. Hans Kelsen, for example, has shown how the concept of the *state* may be reduced to that of *law*, and I think he has shown it fairly satisfactorily. And I think, in the end, it is impossible to keep the concepts of *liberty* and *equality* apart. Certainly, one of the results to be expected from philosophical definition is a greater economy of concepts. And again, the so-called 'idealist' political philosophy has, unlike any other I know, made a genuine attempt to define the concept of the *self* philosophically; and the result has been that those who still cling to the notion that somehow if a philosophical concept is in disagreement with a corresponding commonsense concept it must be wrong, have rejected this philosophy of politics. But if there is any truth in my view of the nature of a philosophy of politics, their rejection may be right, but it is certainly upon false grounds.

However, the illustration I wish to give concerns the *concepts of valuation* involved in the explanation of political activity. Among the concepts which at first glance political life is likely to present to a philosophy of politics for redefinition are some which may be called broadly normative concepts, or concepts of valuation – right and wrong, good and bad, ought and ought not, obligation and duty. These concepts, indeed, take an extremely important place in most attempts to formulate a philosophy of politics. A philosophy of politics commonly resolves itself into the definition of the rest of the presented concepts in terms of one or more of those concepts of valuation, the determination of the end or purpose in political activity. The philosophy of politics is frequently conceived (as we have seen) as the determination of the basis of right of the institution and conditions of political association. The usual procedure appears to be this. First, we discover that political activity, like any activity, presupposes a concept of what is 'good'. Political institutions are conceived as 'ethical ideas'. Secondly, we take over (or if we are particularly conscientious, we think out for ourselves) some definition of the concept 'good' and then apply it to political life. And this is called laying the ethical foundation to our philosophy of politics. Now, whatever there is to be said against this procedure, it seems at any rate impossible to neglect those concepts of valuation altogether. Any attempt to define thoroughly the character of political life is likely to bring us to these concepts, which will appear, in the first place as presuppositions of political activity. But what I want to suggest is that, if this is the direction from which we approach the task of constructing a philosophy of political life, then (i) it is misleading to call this laying the ethical foundation of a philosophy of politics, and (ii) there are *two* steps which must be taken before a philosophy of politics comes in sight.

(i) As I see it, this redefinition of the concepts into which political activity is first analysed by relating them to a moral end or purpose is, if it is at all cogent, not a process of laying a preliminary foundation, but part of, or a stage in, the process by which these concepts are more fully and more satisfactorily defined. It is, as I see it, the beginning of the overbalancing of thought into philosophical thought. And what is produced is not a foundation upon which to build a philosophy of politics, but a philosophy of politics itself of, at any rate, a certain degree of satisfactoriness.

(ii) But my second suggestion is that this is not a point at which it is satisfactory to stop. To stop here is to stop before a genuine philosophy of politics has been achieved. There are, then, from this point of view, two steps to be taken. First, the step by which such concepts as 'government', 'law', 'sovereignty', are transformed and made more concrete by being exhibited from the standpoint of value. This is a real transformation, such as is to be looked for at every stage in this progressive attempt to define more and more comprehensively any set of concepts whatever. To enquire what comprehensive purpose government serves certainly involves a radical change in our concept of government; it involves the redefinition of the concept. And this transformation may be said to have been undertaken by every philosophy of politics of which we need take note – even by that of Hobbes.

But secondly, there is the step by which the criterion of value itself is defined. And it is here that our serious difficulties begin. The criterion of value may be expressed in various ways – for example, in terms of 'good', 'right', or in the more general terms of 'ought'. But each of these expressions indicates a concept with a whole world of presuppositions behind it. They are none of them concrete, categorical concepts. And, as I understand it, it is the business of philosophical thought first to unearth these presuppositions; and secondly to reconstruct the concepts in a more concrete form. In short, it is no doubt true that we get closer to this concrete character of political life when we conceive it in terms of value, but these terms themselves are inherently defective from the standpoint of philosophy and must, in turn, be superseded. These concepts of valuation are never genuinely philosophical concepts. They are based upon presuppositions and are consequently not categorical; they are never fully indicative; and they are not fully and explicitly affirmative. And this task of redefining these concepts of valuation is not a task which can be relegated to 'metaphysics'; it is a task which the actual powers of formulating a philosophy of politics presents, and which a philosophy of politics can refuse to deal with only at the expense of a failure to be purely philosophical.

The transformation of these concepts of valuation which a philosophy must undertake may be expressed in various ways.

The business of philosophical thought here may be said to be the discovery of what is *in* the mind in formative judgements as distinct from what is merely *before* the mind. For example, although the concept of 'self-realization' is, perhaps, unlikely to be before the mind as the criterion in political activity, nevertheless it may be the correct analysis or definition of what is in the mind, it may be the concrete concept which a philosophy of valuation is in need of. What is merely before the mind, and finds explicit expression in the concept of valuation as such, must always fall short of the situation as a whole, the situation viewed from the standpoint of the totality of the experience. Or again, this transformation may be said to be the process by which the ultimate factual basis of right is brought to the surface. A philosophy of politics, we have seen, is frequently represented as the attempt to discover the basis of right for the facts of political life and activity, though it would, I think, be better to say that its task is to transform the concepts involved in political life by relating them to a concept of right. But my view is that it must fall short of a genuine philosophy unless it takes this second step and establishes the ultimate factual basis of right itself or better, transforms the concepts of political life as conceived in terms of right by relating the concept of right itself to the totality of experience. I do not, of course, suggest that a factual basis for right can be found in the same world of fact as that which the concept of right was originally designed to explain. I mean that wherever there is an 'ought' there must be an 'is' presupposed, for a mere 'might' is a meaningless abstraction. I mean that an imperative is more self-explanatory and that consequently a concept involving a mere imperative must be an incompletely defined concept. It has, of course, often been denied that it is possible to find a factual basis for right in any region of fact; it has been asserted both that 'right', and every other so-called 'ethical characteristic', are not further definable. And if this be true, then something like a philosophy of politics would be the result merely of redefining the concepts of political life in terms of a concept of valuation. But the view I am suggesting is that these concepts of valuation are incompletely defined concepts because they are not in the highest degree categorical, affirmative and indicative, that (consequently) merely to redefine the concepts of political life in terms of these cannot itself constitute a philosophy of politics, and that the business of a philosophy of politics is to persevere with this task of continual redefinition of concepts until a comprehensively concrete result is achieved.

Now, the common objection to this view, and the objection to the kind of philosophy of politics it implies, is that this philosophy of politics would involve the complete transformation of these concepts of valuation, which would no longer be considered adequate for the explanation of political life and activity. It would involve the destruction of the specifically normative character of these concepts; an imperative would be transformed into an indicative, an 'ought' to an 'is'. But this objection seems to me beside the mark. Unless such a transformation does take place, I am suggesting nothing like a philosophy can appear, because nothing like a concrete concept has appeared. If this transformation is possible, then it must be carried out, and it is pointless to object to it merely on the grounds that it is a transformation. The theory of punishment affords an illustration of what I mean. As it stands in most attempts to formulate a philosophy of politics, the concept of punishment is conceived in moral terms. The question discussed is, 'What basis in right is there for punishment?' Punishment is explained and defined in terms of what is taken to be the moral end of the state. But, as I understand it, both crime and punishment must be defined in some more concrete way before a philosophically satisfactory definition is achieved. We must not only get away from the merely negative concept of crime and punishment which seems to satisfy some thinkers, but we must also get beyond the merely usual concept of crime and punishment to a concept in terms of ultimate fact. Whatever its defects, the strength of Hegel's concept of crime as self-contradictory activity and of punishment as the resolution of the contradiction is that it, at least, makes an attempt to transcend the inadequacy and the incoherence of a theory in terms of mere value. It is an attempt to show the concepts of crime and punishment as logically involved in one another, and not merely an attempt to justify crime being followed by punishment in the empirical world. Value is represented as one form of coherence; the mere 'ought' is transformed into an 'is'.

The point, then, that I want to emphasize is that in philosophy, and consequently in a philosophy of politics, the criterion is never conformity with our ordinary view of the matter. Indeed, it must be expected that a philosophy will conflict at every point with what appears to be the commonsense view, because a merely commonsense view must be expected to be incomplete. Indeed, the whole point of philosophy is to get at something more coherent than commonsense gives us. And to suggest that a philosophy of politics must conform to the facts of political life is to suggest that a fully thought-out concept must conform to a concept which we have not troubled to think out at all. And a philosophy of politics must also be expected to conflict with many of the refinements which the merely commonsense view suffers in the course of redefinition. For example, what may be called the purely legal view is one which presents itself continuously to a philosophy of politics, but it is a view which, in the end, reveals its own incompleteness and calls for supersession. Neither to the criminal, nor to the ordinary man is crime likely to appear as self-contradictory activity, but this is no reason for rejecting this definition of the concept. Again, all moral judgement whatever may take the form of a reference of a situation to a rule of action, good always appearing as 'what is my duty', but this is no reason for rejecting the view that, in the last analysis, moral judgement is the reference of a situation to an end, or the view that moral judgement is a judgement with regard to the coherence of life involved in acting or living in a particular way. And once more, the notion of a 'general will' may be something which never occurs to consciousness in political activity of any kind, but it may nevertheless be the ultimate definition of what is present in consciousness, and certainly it must not be rejected as false merely because it cannot be shown to be present to consciousness in political activity.

Now, if this be the character of a philosophy of politics, there are clearly many purposes which it will not, and cannot, serve. It will not, and cannot, give us a view acceptable to commonsense of the purpose and end in political life. It will not give us a view of political life in terms of purpose and end at all. Not only is it useless to expect from a philosophy of politics any explicit judgement about what ought to be the end in political activity; but the whole notion of political life as activity for the achievement of certain ends is superseded by a view of political life in relation to the totality of experience. Activity implies change, and change an identity which does not change; and, as I understand it, the business of philosophy is to conceive change and activity, not merely as what they are for commonsense – more change and activity – but concretely, as abstract aspects of a genuine, and therefore changeless, totality.

And a philosophy of politics is an attempt to get away from what political life appears to be for commonsense – activity for the achievement of some end – to a view of the character of political life from the concrete standpoint of the totality of experience. A philosophy of politics, then, is unable to give guidance for action, and it cannot be supposed to fail as a philosophy because it fails to give guidance for action. It is not itself a political programme; it is not a foundation or basis, a body of general principles upon which a political programme might be constructed. It is concerned with the ultimate, not merely the psychological and ethical, presuppositions of political beliefs, actions and institutions, and is the attempt to reformulate the concepts of political life so that they include those presuppositions. Or, more comprehensively, it is what occurs when the attempt – common to all forms of political thought – to define the concepts of political life is carried out with unqualified freedom, but is pressed to an ultimate conclusion.

When we turn back again to Hobbes, I think we can find there something like a genuine philosophy of politics in this sense. Of course there is much else besides, and the philosophy is not always satisfactorily distinguished from what does not pretend to be philosophical analysis. And again, I think, in spite of serious defects, there is also to be found in Hegel's *Philosophy of Right* a genuine philosophy of politics, conceived as I have suggested it should be conceived. Where else a philosophy of politics is to be found, I should not like to say. But these are questions into which we need not go. My suggestion is, simply, that the concept of a philosophy of politics which is implied in a great many, if not most, political theories which pretend to be philosophical is unsatisfactory, because it, in effect, denies a genuinely philosophical character to the philosophy of politics; and that I think I can see a way of conceiving a philosophy of politics which does not commit this elementary mistake, and which gives meaning to much of what such writers as Hobbes and Hegel have to say which otherwise would be difficult to understand.

POLITICAL PHILOSOPHY

1946–50

I

When one reflects upon anything – on poetry, on the weather, or on the civil service – one makes an assumption which it is the precise purpose of the reflection to question or even to deny. All reflection begins with something assumed to be known, but in reflection what is assumed to be known is assumed also not to be known. We begin with knowledge which is nevertheless assumed to be ignorance. Reflection, for example, may be directed upon the determination of the character of something: but *what* we reflect upon already has a character imputed to it, it is recognized as *something*, that is, it is assumed to be known; but the reason for our reflection is the opposite assumption, that what we take to be 'knowledge' is infected with ignorance. The root from which all reflection springs is the paradox that we know and that at the same time we do not know – a paradox which, as we shall see, is not to be resolved by describing our situation as one of knowing but of not knowing *enough* and of wanting to know *more*.

That reflection begins from knowledge, and not from sheer ignorance, scarcely needs arguing. Mere ignorance implies a vacancy of mind impossible of achievement. 'I never', says Hume, 'catch myself without a perception'. Nevertheless, the notion that reflection can protect itself against error only if it has its spring in ignorance is not easily suppressed, and some who are willing to concede that absolute ignorance affords no starting-place will be found clinging to the view that the spring of reflection must be in something that falls short of knowledge properly so-called. The name given to this neutral spring of reflection (something that is neither knowledge nor ignorance), is 'observation' or (more simply) 'experience.' But this, like absolute ignorance, is only the fancy of a deluded mind. Admittedly the disorder and inconsequence of our first-knowledge is pre-eminent, and seems to make the enterprise of reflection a difficult one; but it is a difficulty not to be avoided, denying it the character of knowledge. If, then, human beings were absolutely ignorant, it is impossible to see how they could ever reflect or ever acquire knowledge. And if it were possible to enjoy an experience of mere 'observation', it is impossible to see how knowledge could ever spring from it. The condition of acquiring knowledge is having it already. But further, if human beings were satisfied with the knowledge they already possessed, there would be no room for further reflection. In short, reflection presupposes doubt, but not universal doubt. These very obvious remarks may, perhaps, be summed up by saying that the process in reflection is *dialectical*, a process of considering something recognized as knowledge and supposed to be true, yet considering it with the assumption that it is not true – an assumption which we sometimes improperly interpret as 'not wholly true' or 'not the whole truth'.

2

This I believe to be, not merely the character of one peculiar kind of reflection, but the universal character of all reflection. Unless we reflect there is no world; and when we reflect we engage in this dialectical activity.

For example, to reflect upon the history of England is to reflect upon that amorphous collection of opinion we call our knowledge of the history of England. The knowledge with which the historian begins is, not only his newly gathered discoveries (if he has made any), but is also the history of England as he learned it in the nursery. In reflection, no doubt, the whole of his knowledge, including his own discoveries, is criticized and transformed; but the historian begins neither with ignorance nor with mere observation, but with a world of ideas, a history of England.

Or again, scientific reflection is reflection upon opinions – in the main upon opinions about relations, about causes and effects. Scientific knowledge does not spring from blank ignorance, or from something called 'observation'; it is the complex product of a manner of reflection in which knowledge gives rise to hypothesis, hypothesis calls for test, and test issues in more significant knowledge. It is a dialectical process in which neither absolute ignorance nor certain knowledge has any place.

3

Reflective enterprises, then, are not distinguished from one another in respect of what I have called their dialectical character. This belongs to their common nature. They share the general presupposition of knowledge infected with ignorance. Among these enterprises, however, an important distinction may be observed between those which involve only a partial subversion of the 'knowledge' with which they begin, and that which is radically subversive.

Subversion in some degree belongs, of course, to the character of all reflection – the subversion of the knowledge with which reflection begins. And this subversion, even when its range is limited, may go very deep. The historian may reach the conclusion that there were two St Patricks, living at widely different times, who have got themselves confused as one; or he may conclude that there never was a St Patrick at all. These, and other, conclusions are, of course, the results of reformulating opinions about the significance of other opinions. And further, when once the knowledge with which the historian begins has submitted to the first subversive touches of reflection, there is no means of arresting the process of subversion; the reformulation of one detail is the reformulation of the whole. Nevertheless the historian, without denying the contagious character of reformulation, will always feel himself to be reaching back to something indissoluble, which he will call 'the evidence'. And he will consider it no part of his enterprise to subvert 'the evidence'. The historian of the English Parliament, for example, may know that what he reflects upon is recorded human opinions, but Parliament as a generalization, as a generalization not of human opinions but of human activities, comes to him with a compelling unity which is difficult, if not impossible, to deny; and his history may be driven into the form of a history of an institution. He knows that what he is reflecting upon is not merely the meaning of the word 'Parliament', and he easily takes this to imply that he is dealing with material firmer and less fluid than opinions.

This limit of subversion is sometimes spoken of as the point at which reflection escapes from the world of *opinions* into a world of *facts* and *things*. For the historian those 'things' are what the evidence is about; for the natural scientist they compose his natural world which is the subject of scientific opinion. And once you have got back to a *fact* or a *thing*, reflection can be represented as getting to know more about *it*, or as adding to a knowledge of *it*. Bacon thought of our knowledge of the natural world in this manner, and consequently conceived the necessity of a method appropriate to deal with the truth of things, parallel to the already developed method for dealing with the truth of opinions. This, of course, is an unfortunate way of thinking of the situation: *facts* and *things* are not another world from the world of opinions; they are merely relatively unshakable opinions. Nevertheless, a reflective enterprise which includes in its assumptions the presupposition that it is possible to establish a body of opinion so firmly that it can be given the name of 'fact' or 'thing', is clearly a kind of reflection in which subversion has an actual or a potential limit. Facts may be merely very well established opinions; but if and when they are established they become an unquestioned part of knowledge, and the reflective enterprise takes on the appearance of building a structure upon an assured foundation, of getting to know *more* about something whose identity (indeed, whose character) is in some way already fixed. And, as in the case of 'Parliament,' the historian may be in a position to believe himself to *start* with a 'fact' which his own reflection has had no hand in making.

In reflection, then, there are occasions when an arbitrary (but not necessarily an unconsidered) term is put to subversiveness: landmarks are set up, firm anchorages are laid out, with the intention of fixing limits beyond which reflection shall not stray. But a reflective enterprise which had the precise purpose of avoiding all such fixed points of reference, one designed to remain fluid, one for which no presupposition was sacred, would not improperly be called *radically subversive*. This, I believe, is the distinguishing characteristic of philosophical reflection. And on this account it is exceedingly difficult to compose a brief definition of philosophy. For if we call it 'the continuous and relentless criticism of all the assumptions of human knowledge', we must somehow avoid the suggestion that 'human knowledge' is something fixed, *about* which the philosopher is anxious to learn something *more* than he already knows. In both historical and scientific reflection, for example, there are pauses when, some temporary identity having been recognized, reflection becomes centered upon the identity, the historian or scientist seeking to know more about *it*. But in radically subversive reflection this can never happen. Nor could philosophy thus conceived ever reach unassailable conclusions: the project of Lucius Gellius, who, Cicero tells us, offered his good offices as an arbitrator in the philosophical disputes of the Athenians, was appropriate to a different sort of philosophy.

That the starting-place of philosophy is the same as that of any other reflective enterprise – knowledge infected with ignorance – will not be felt to be a handicap. But the view that philosophical reflection is radically dialectical has been the cause of some misgiving. Reflection which could never at any point hope to support that blessed transformation inaugurated by the appearance of a certainty (however modest or atten- uated) upon which more ample certainties could be raised, is surely condemned to move in a profitless circle; and those who engage in this sort of reflection may be expected to come out at the same door as they went in, and without the satisfaction of having made any certainly valuable purchases on the way. It is not, then, surprising that some of those who have felt this misgiving must actually have sought a way out of the difficulty. But to see it as a difficulty to be overcome or an imperfection to be removed is only to have discovered a lack of interest in radically subversive reflection; it cannot be taken to deny its possibility. The Cartesian project of transforming philosophy by setting a limit to the subversion permitted, and the positivist project of achieving the same purpose by approximating phil- osophy to natural science, are to be deprecated not for what they have achieved (because, of course, they have achieved something), but for what they deny – the significance, or even the possibility, of radically subversive reflection.

4

Let me, inspired by a passage in a book which recently came my way, present all this to you in a figure.

The enterprise in reflection may be likened to ascending a

tower liberally supplied with windows at every level. The world seen from the ground floor is the world with which all reflection begins. But as we climb, the scene changes: the ascent brings into view what was before invisible, and at each new level a new world appears. Now, within the corners of this figure, it might be suggested that different forms of the reflective enterprise are distinguished from one another merely in respect of the height to which the climber is disposed to climb, the philosopher being prepared to go on where the others are content to stop. But this, though it may give some insight into the character of reflection, is not the primary ground of the distinction between philosophy and other (less subversive) forms of the reflective enterprise. What at bottom distinguishes different forms of reflection is *not* the willingness or unwillingness to continue to climb, but the willingness or unwillingness of the thinker to carry with him to higher levels the fixed and remembered relics of the view as it appeared at a lower level, the willingness or unwillingness to allow what was once seen to determine a later vision. The important distinction is between the thinker for whom the different levels of observation provide different views of 'things' already known, and the thinker who, as it were, uninfluenced by memory and carrying nothing with him as he climbs, knows at each level only the scene presented to his vision and the mediation by which it came into view. For example, at the ground level the historian may see and identify a church, a town hall, a market-place and a battle, and however high into the tower he climbs he will always regard himself as being presented at each new level with a wider, or more related, or more reliable view of what he saw in the beginning: the significance of the battle may change, but the battle always remains a battle. Philosophical reflection, on the other hand, is what happens when the kind of anchorage is rejected, each scene being permitted fully to supersede the one before. This, perhaps, will make the philosopher specially eager to continue his ascent, just as the historian will be disposed to stop at the highest level at which the scene retains its familiarity for him. Nevertheless, the essential difference does not lie in the height attained, but in the predisposition of the climber. There is no top to this tower, or at least the philosopher has no means of knowing whether or not he has reached the top; for others there will be an optimum level beyond which the 'things' to which this vision clings dissolve. The philosopher just does his best; and the cogency of his reflection will be revealed, not only in the impetus of his ascent, but also in his ability to disclose the manner and the intermediary of the process in which one scene supersedes another. That is, he is a philosopher not in respect to something he achieves at the end, but in respect of his predisposition towards the ascent. Indeed, it might be said that his only tangible achievement is the maintenance of this predisposition. Thus, philosophy may be thought of as unhindered reflective enterprise; we should all be philosophers were we not liable to be distracted by what we first saw.

5

Now, political philosophy is reflective enterprise having its starting place in political experience; it is the unhindered reflective impulse making itself manifest in connection with the kind of activity we call politics. As in other reflective enterprises, we begin here with something of which we assert that 'we know what it is'. We all know what politics are. And yet it is just because we do not know, because we are uncertain, doubtful, that we reflect. We begin with knowledge which we suspect to be ignorance.

What do we know? What is the appearance of politics when it just comes into view? For this is where we are to begin. But once again we must pause to get clear the significance of this question before trying to answer it. Philosophers, in the belief that it is important to be confident that the starting-place of reflection possesses qualities such as simplicity or unambiguity, urge us to take pains to assure ourselves that this 'past view' is unencumbered by second thoughts or the relics of undetected sophistication. But this, I think, is itself a relic of the error that it is desirable (or even possible) to begin with something certain, an experience that involves no theory, or to begin with a blank sheet. The question, what do politics look like when we first perceive them? does not mean, what is the scientific minimum we can say about politics when we have purged our perceptions of the contingencies and irrelevancies of informal observation? It means merely, what did we learn about politics in the nursery?

Politics, it appears, are a form of practical human activity; they are practical activity concerned in the arrangements of a society. Those who engage in this activity seem to be moved by a desire to impose upon the human world as they find it a character which it does not already possess. The conduct of policy is the human world seen in relation to our desires. This is clearly so when the aim of policy is to inaugurate change. But it is not less so when the world is very much as we desire it to be and policy is devoted to its maintenance; for to maintain is actively to resist one change by inaugurating another change.

In its attitude, then, political activity is not initially distinguished from other forms of practical activity. The world which consists of what is good to eat and what is poisonous, the world in which the sea incites to navigation and the earth to cultivation, a world in which everything exists to be made use of, is the world of politics. 'We must have spent three hours', says a writer recalling a visit to the Owen Falls, Lake Victoria, 'watching the waters and resolving plans to harness and bridle them. So much power running to waste, such a coign of vantage unoccupied, such a lever to control the natural forces of Africa ungripped cannot but vex and stimulate the imagination.' The dominion over the things of the earth first given to man is the root of all political activity.

But Augustine was not in error when he perceived that some additional circumstance was required to make politics spring from his root. Politics are practical activity concerned with the relations of human beings to one another, and though the relations of human beings to the things of the earth can never be securely insulated from their relations to one another, they are never the primary considerations in politics; the organization of human beings to things is always subordinate to the organization of human beings to each other. Nevertheless, the attitude in politics towards human beings and their relations to one another is a practical attitude; the relations are regarded as material upon which a character, perhaps an orderly character, is to be imposed. In politics every person is known as the consumer of what I produce, the producer of what I consume, one way or another the partner in a common project. At best in politics we live for mutual improvement.

The remote, universal spring of human conduct may be called appetite or energy. This formless, limitless *wanting* is never actually experienced: what we experience is an educated want — a want turned into a wish capable of satisfaction. Social life — the life of human beings — is to be conscious that some desires are approved and others disapproved. The problem in conduct is how to secure the satisfaction of approved desires.

The concrete expression of this approval, and the arrangements by which the satisfaction of what is approved is achieved, are to be found in customs, in laws and in institutions. Politics, briefly, are the means by which the institutional expression of approval and disapproval is adjusted to the gradual shift of judgement, and the means by which the integrity of the methods of satisfaction is preserved. Always and everywhere they are an activity of modification: an existing order of approved desires and achieved satisfactions is the starting-place in politics, and what we desire to impose is already hidden in what exists.

Now, if some critic is roused to exclaim that all this is itself the product of reflection (though not, perhaps, of very profound reflection), that it is already replete with theory, and that it is, moreover, questionable if not actually false – I would not for a moment deny it: these are the characteristics of all possible starting-places of reflection. Find, if you wish, another beginning. I insist only that you will search in vain for a starting-place either in the blank sheet of ignorance or in an 'observation' untouched by reflection. And if I claim no particular virtue in this starting-place, you, no doubt, will allow me the liberty of beginning here. And the question I wish to consider is, what are we to expect from those who direct their powers of reflection upon politics? For somewhere among these we may hope to find a political philosopher.

6

The first answer we must give to this question is that what we should properly expect will depend upon the mode of the reflection. And if we consider the world of political reflection which current writing presents to us, we may distinguish in it at least three different kinds of reflection, each of which, if we understand its nature, should rouse in us an expectation peculiar to itself. I do not assert that reflection in politics is confined within these limits; indeed, I know it is not. I take these three merely by way of illustration.

(a) The first kind of reflection may be called reflection *in the service of politics*. When one turns his reflective impulse upon the arrangements of his society and considers the degree in which they afford satisfaction to the desires approved in his society, his reflection may be said to be in the service of politics. And we may properly expect from such reflection some recommendations about the political ends which should be pursued, and the means which should be used to attain those ends. The result of such reflection is *policy*, something designed to control political activity. Now, this sort of reflection in the service of politics may, clearly, exist at a variety of levels of coherence; and it is clear also that political activity is impossible without it. But from our point of view its most noticeable characteristic is the absence from it of the radically subversive impulse. However revolutionary it may be in practical detail, reflectively it involves only a small degree of subversion. It is a reflective enterprise in which belief and opinion rapidly assume the appearance of 'fact', and in which the greatest handicap is to be without a body of fixed and reliable 'certainties'. And to disturb these 'certainties' will be as remote from the purpose of this kind of reflection as it is remote from the enterprise of the carpenter to concentrate his mind upon the reconstruction of a tool while he is working with it, or of the chess-player to invent new pieces while he is engaged in playing a game.

(b) The second kind of reflection on politics is distinguished from the first in respect of its aim: its purpose is not to *determine* political activity, but to give a certain sort of *explanation* of political activity. It is reflective enterprise turned towards the construction of what I shall call a *political doctrine*.

The conduct of policy itself, however firmly it may be controlled by reflection, is unavoidably a relatively disordered affair. Powerful desires are thwarted by adverse circumstances; plans go astray; and a well-found project becomes a drifting hulk, a prey to every current, merely because some fortuitous occurrence stole its wind. But when a society, over a long period, has achieved a settled manner of existence, and when circumstances have permitted policy to hold a steady course, an almost self-conscious coherence or uniformity of character is generated. And when the reflective impulse is directed to the detection and exploration of this character, extrapolating its tendencies, fixing its elements, and making firm its outline, the result is a *political doctrine*. Indeed, such a doctrine may spring not only from an actual, but also from an imaginary political experience. Whatever offers opportunity for analysis and more orderly reconstruction may be expected to feel the touch of this explanatory device. Feudalism, mercantilism and Fascism are examples of such doctrines sprung from actual political experience; syndicalism may serve as an example of a doctrine sprung from imaginary political experience.

At first sight it might appear that, so far from representing political activity (actual or imaginary), doctrines of this kind are nothing but misrepresentations of the experience from which they spring. But this, I think, is not all there is to be said of them. It is true that, in a doctrine of this kind, political activity appears in a greatly abridged and simplified form. The reflective effort to understand and to explain results in a *reductio ad unum* which, for example, makes it worthless to the historian except as material. Who would go to the seventeenth-century inventors of 'feudalism' for a knowledge of how a feudal society in the Middle Ages actually lived? Nevertheless, a doctrine of this kind has an explanatory value, which springs precisely from its being a *reductio ad absurdum* of a political experience. By representing as actual what is, in experience, only potential, by reducing individuals to types, by simplifying the outline and approximating the details to one another – all of which may not improperly be described as a *reductio ad absurdum* – a political doctrine may reveal the nature of a political experience in the same way as the over-emphasis of caricature reveals the potentialities of a face and a parody the potentialities of a style.

As a reflective enterprise, the construction of a political doctrine is clearly more subversive than reflection merely in the service of political activity. But it clearly also falls far short of being radically subversive. Reflection here may throw down some familiar landmarks, dissolve men into social classes and events into processes, and it may make the world of political activity not readily recognizable to men actually engaged in that activity; but for every 'certainty' it displaces it offers another in return. It is incapable of throwing off entirely its allegiance to the political experience from which it springs; it never loses its character of being an explanation *of* something whose character is already fixed. Just as in the grammar book of our language we learn for the first time of verbs and nouns and adjectives and yet recognize this as knowledge about 'things' we know before but without knowing their class-names, so a political doctrine is never so subversive as to represent itself as anything other than knowledge of an already familiar political world. A political doctrine may be expected to help us to recognize a style of politics when we come upon it, as an architectural handlook may be expected to improve our powers of recognizing a style of building when we seen an example of it, but more it cannot do.

As explanation, then, a political doctrine of this kind has a characteristic and limited value; it is an undeniable attempt to make politics intelligible. It springs from a reflective enterprise which is neither to be despised nor overrated. But when, as so often happens, it is converted to the service of political activity and is given the task of guiding policy, its very virtues prevent it from supplying what is expected of it. It is not, perhaps, impossible for a society to conduct its affairs successfully under the guidance of a political doctrine of this sort, but if it does so, it will be by chance. There is on record a case of a man cured of a dangerous illness by eating his doctor's prescription which he understood was the medicine itself, but he cannot be said to have been anything but a lucky man: the cure can scarcely be assigned to the treatment. And the degree of subversiveness in the reflective enterprise which terminates in a political doctrine is such as to make the doctrine a necessarily false guide in political activity. We should expect, then, enlightenment of a certain sort, but no practical guidance from this kind of explanatory reflection on politics.

(c) Now, I have not forgotten that the matter before us is the determination of the character of political philosophy. Indeed, I embarked upon this study of reflective enterprise making itself manifest in connection with politics in the hope of finding hidden in it something that could properly be called philosophical reflection in politics. We know in general what we are looking for – reflection connected with politics in which the invitation inherent in all reflection, the invitation to become radically subversive, is accepted without reserve. We know that we should not find what we are looking for in the activity of those who search the body of their political 'knowledge' in order to unearth some element or suggestion of certainty, of 'fact', which, were it so detected, can be used as a foundation upon which to raise an edifice of larger and more impressive certainties. In philosophy, to be hot for certainty is always a mistake, and to be so at the beginning is a fatal mistake. So far, then, we have come upon reflective enterprises in connection with politics which refuse the invitation to become radically subversive. Indeed, this virtue and value lies precisely in this refusal. And if we had time to explore further the ranges of reflection on politics, and came upon something that was genuinely scientific in character, as well we might, we shall find here also a similar refusal of the invitation to radical subversiveness.

From reflection in the service of politics we may expect, at best, a *policy*, some more or less coherent view, based upon the current notions of what is desirable to be pursued and upon the current practical knowledge and sympathies of the society, of how we ought to act. From reflection which aims at giving a firm, if narrow, intelligibility to political experience, we may expect a *doctrine*. These are reflective enterprises the work of which lies in an achieved result; and since a conclusion is sought, a term is put to the impetus of reflection. But philosophical reflection is distinguished from those offering, not only a different focus for our expectations, but a focus of an altogether different kind. The only assured achievement in political philosophy is the maintenance, in the face of innumerable temptations to abandon it, of this attitude of radical reflective subversiveness. This is what makes it 'philosophical'; and when reflection loses its impetus, and falls back upon the enterprise of exploring the character of something whose character is assumed to be, wholly or in part, fixed, it becomes mechanical and ceases to be philosophical. The aim in philosophical reflection is to think philosophically, not to construct a 'philosophy'.

Now, there is little doubt that even those who are disposed to be sympathetic towards this conception of political philosophy will find in what I have said only a very meager determination of its character. To say that political philosophy is what happens when, in the enjoyment of a political experience, the potential subversiveness of reflection is allowed to have its way without hindrance or arrest, is not, perhaps, to have said very much. Nevertheless, it is precisely this which seems to me to distinguish Plato's *Republic*, Hobbes's *Leviathan*, Spinoza's *Ethics* and Hegel's *Grundlinien der Philosophie des Rechts*. If we read these works in order to extract from them a philosophical teaching, we shall not go away empty-handed. But if we read them as masterpieces of philosophical reflection, in order to observe how a genuine philosopher conducts his business, we shall go away with something much more valuable. For, paradoxically enough, it is easier to construct a political philosophy than to hold fast to the enterprise of thinking philosophically, and what distinguishes the masterpiece is the second and more difficult achievement.

We ought, of course, to consider the difficulties which this view of the character of political philosophy involves; but any other manner of determining it will, I think, be found to involve us in the necessity of reservations and qualifications which in the end bring us back to this determination. For example, I would be prepared to accept the view that the impulse in political philosophy is the impulse to detect *the permanent character of political activity*. This seems to be a not unfair description of the enterprise of Plato, of Augustine or of Aquinas; and when a philosopher tries to extract, from the way in which people talk and act, the assumptions they are working on, he is making a modest beginning enterprise. But before I will fully accept this description of the enterprise I should want to be certain that the phrase 'the permanent character of political activity'[1] was not understood in such a manner as to suggest that there is something fixed and familiar, called 'political activity', and that our knowledge of it had only to be enlarged, extended or increased in order to become philosophical knowledge. Here, as anywhere else, what *it* is depends upon the circumstances in which it is considered. 'If the environment of a stone is the adjacent spaces, then the *it* of the stone is the occupation of a certain space. If its environment is the bodies upon which it presses, then the *it* is pressure.'[2] The permanent political activity is not merely an extension and enlargement of what we are just acquainted with; the permanent *it* is what it *becomes* when given a place in an intelligible universe. Or again, to say that the purpose in political philosophy is to recognize the activity in politics in its place on the map of the intelligible universe, is unobjectionable only so long as the character of political activity is not identified, or assumed to have been identified, in advance of determining its place on the map. But perhaps the least objectionable figure is that of a text and a context, where the purpose in reflection is to determine the meaning; because the meaning is not something which belongs to the text or to the context, neither of which is fixed independently of the other, but is properly assumed to be in the unity which text and context together compose, and in which, as text and context, they cease to exist. Political philosophy, then, as I see it, is saying something concerned with political activity such that, if true, things will

[1] G.C. Field, *Principles and Ideals in Politics*.
[2] Nettleship, *Remains*. I. 33.

be as they are; not as they were when we first caught sight of them, but as they permanently are. And here, as elsewhere, we must embark upon the enterprise itself if we wish to come to a clear understanding of it; there is no way of determining the end until it is achieved.

7

Now, the greatest difficulty in philosophical reflection is to throw off the allegiance, which continually forces itself upon us, to so-called 'fact'. As the philosopher ascends the tower of reflection, he is at every step reminded of the view he has enjoyed at a lower level; and this view presents itself to him as a criterion, as something achieved and settled, to which subsequent perceptions must conform. Each new level gives what unavoidably tends to be recognized as a new view of something seen before. And our accustomed ways of speaking of the enterprise reinforce the pull of this false allegiance. We speak of reflection *on* or *about* something, and thereby inadvertently attribute the character of a foundation to what is really only a starting-place. And all this is particularly true in political philosophy, which so easily comes to be thought of as philosophical reflection *on* political activity. Indeed, it seems that if the force of this expression 'philosophical reflection *on* political activity' is weakened, nothing remains to prevent political philosophy from being swept into the general undifferentiated stream of philosophical reflection, there to lose its identity; its anchorage in political activity seems to be its only claim to distinction, and, in consequence, it seems to be condemned to be philosophical in only a qualified sense. Nevertheless the appearance is, I believe deceptive; a standing-ground for political philosophy may be found which does not entail any weakening of the resolve, inseparable from every kind of philosophical reflection, to deny the character of permanent 'fact' to what is only the view we have enjoyed from an arbitrary starting-point or a temporary stopping-place – the resolve to put no restriction upon the dialectic of reflection. In the first place, political philosophy is clearly distinguished in virtue of its spring in the world of politics: the 'knowledge' which is its starting-place is political knowledge. The enterprise in philosophy is to spread one's sails to the reflective impulse; in political philosophy it is to do this starting from a mooring-place of political experience. But if this were all, the thread which attaches political philosophy to political activity would be tenuous and soon broken – indeed, it would be the avowed purposes of political philosophy to break it. And the thread once broken, and the mooring-place soon out of sight and out of mind, political philosophy on the high seas of reflection would be indistinguishable from philosophical enterprises emanating from other ports of origin – from religious, from scientific or from artistic experience. But this is not quite all that is to be said. If to break the thread that attaches it to its mooring, if to remain unencumbered by our allegiance to what was first perceived or to what was perceived at a lower level, is the first task in philosophical reflection, there is a second and not less significant task – to explore and to record that process of mediation by which the scene at one level passes into the scene at another and higher level. And a philosophical enterprise remains attached to the experience from which it sprang, not because of a fettering allegiance to what is left behind, but on account of what may be described as a continuous voyage. A reflective enterprise which, though relieved of the necessity of conforming itself at every moment to its starting-place, is nevertheless hindered by no hiatus, is an enterprise at once free from the spell which the already perceived casts on present perceptions and one which retains a connection with the experience from which it sprang, a connection which continues to determine its character. In philosophy, reflection does not mount on wings, careless of the stages of ascent; it must be able constantly to rehearse the steps by which it rises and it must be at home on every level. Political philosophy, then, may be said to be the genuine, unhindered impulse of reflection, setting out from a political experience, and keeping faith with the original experience, not by continuous conformity to it, but by reason of an unbroken descent. This, I believe, is the principle of the One and the Many in all forms of philosophical reflection.

8

There is, however, one conclusion from which all this which, because it is difficult to swallow, will be thought to discredit the premise: the conclusion that we must expect from political philosophy no practical political conclusions whatever. Political philosophy can provide no principles to be 'followed', no rules of political conduct to be observed, no ideals of policy or arrangement to be pursued. Now, I am not concerned to defend a political philosophy which cannot provide these things against the charge that it is clearly a waste of time; I want only to make more convincing the character of a political philosophy which cannot provide them.

In one sense, no doubt, all reflective activity is practical. The subversion of a given world of experience is, certainly, *doing* something, it is generating a change, and on this account it is practical. And if philosophical reflection is radically subversive reflection, it cannot avoid being in this general sense, practical. But this general view must be qualified, or we shall find ourselves committed to the absurd conclusion that philosophical reflection (because it is the most subversive kind of reflection) is of all reflective enterprises the most pre-eminently practical, that the conduct of policy itself is the least practical kind of reflection because it involves the least amount of reflective subversion of its material.

Beyond the practical character common to all reflective enterprise we may, then, detect a narrower and more precise practical character peculiar to a reflective enterprise concerned pre-eminently with the realization of desires in the world of existing events; 'desires', of course, being understood to be ideas and 'existing events' to be other ideas to which desire gives a relative fixity of character in order to have a world in which to realize itself. To accept the world more or less as it just appears, and to rearrange the detail of that appearance so as to make it correspond with our desires is a practical activity in this narrow, precise sense. For example, the scientist reflecting upon the nature of heat and cold is setting about the reflective subversion of a given world of experience, and in this sense his activity is practical even if no attempt is made to apply the results of this reflection to the conduct of life. But the activity of a man, who, feeling himself to be cold, sets about the transformation of his world in order to get warmer (for example, by shutting the window), is practical not only in the general and inevitable sense but also in this other and more precise sense. It is practical because it involves a knowledge of heat and cold in the service of the satisfaction of desire and involves therefore a knowledge of heat and cold springing from a kind of reflection which is limited to the pursuit of this end.

Now, politics, the promotion or recommendation of change

in existing political arrangements, are a practical activity in the precise sense; they are activity in which reflective enterprise is necessarily limited. And a mode of reflection which is to provide principles or rules (or indeed anything at all) relevant to politics must share the limitations of this character. But this is exactly what is impossible to political philosophy so long as it retains its character of radically subversive reflection. Where in reflection fixed points of reference are demanded as a condition of the profitableness of the reflection, a demand has been made for the arrest of the reflective impulse – a demand which, *ex hypothesi*, political philosophy must refuse. And if we expect from political philosophy conclusions relevant to politics, the result will be either a political philosophy in which the reflective impulse is hindered and arrested by being made servile to politics, or a political activity in which the reflective impulse, disengaged from the necessary limits of politics, has lost its virtue. Where there is genuine philosophy there can be no guidance; if we seek guidance, we must 'hang up philosophy'.

And it is in the light of this principle that I think we should interpret the writings of the political philosophers. Indeed only an inattentive reader of these writings will be encouraged with other expectations. It is true that Plato, Aquinas or Hobbes sometimes appear to concern themselves with the world of practical politics and appear to regard it as part of their business to make recommendations about the arrangements of society. But the appearance is deceptive, and the deception is not difficult to explain. Institutions and arrangements in the pages of these writers (the philosopher-king of Plato's *Republic*, the monarch of Aquinas, or Hobbes's sovereign) are not recommended as kings to be established, and therefore properly to be considered in respect of their desirability; they are the emblems of philosophical ideas, and therefore not properly considered in respect of their desirability or their practicability or in respect of any other quality or characteristic of the world of practical politics. Wherever there is genuinely philosophical reflection something is being said, such that if true, things will be as they permanently are – that is, as they are *not* in the world of practical politics. And if this seems to be a severe conclusion, it is at least not wantonly severe; it is a conclusion that springs directly from the character I have attributed to political philosophy.

SELECT BIBLIOGRAPHY

Bibliographical Note

Michael Oakeshott minimized footnote references in both his published and his unpublished writings. When he offers footnotes they are characteristically barebones. He thought that a little of this went a long way. He cared about getting his thinking across, and he downplayed grounding philosophic conversation in scholarship. His essays here are presented as he wrote them. The list below provides the details he omitted to aid first-time readers, and those who wish to pursue the background of his thought in greater depth.

Arthur James Balfour, Earl of Balfour, *Theism and Humanism, being the Gifford Lectures delivered at the University of Glasgow, 1914* (New York: Hodder and Stoughton, 1915).

Sir Ernest Barker, *The Study of Political Science and Its Relation to Cognate Studies* (Cambridge University Press, 1928).

Bernard Bosanquet, *The Philosophical Theory of the State* (London and New York: Macmillan, 1899).

Bernard Bosanquet, *The Principle of Individuality and Value, the Gifford Lectures for 1911, delivered in Edinburgh University* (London: Macmillan, 1912).

Bernard Bosanquet, *Social and International Ideals; being studies in patriotism* (London: Macmillan and Co. Ltd, 1917).

Joseph Butler, 'Upon Forgiveness of Injuries', Sermon IX in Volume II of Bishop Butler's *Works: Sermons by the Right Reverend Father in God Joseph Butler, D.C.L., Late Lord Bishop of Durham* (Oxford: At the University Press, MDCCCL), pp. 99–113.

G. D. H. Cole, *Self-government in Industry*, 3rd ed. (London: G. Bell, 1918).

Robert Alexander Duff, *Spinoza's Ethics and Political Philosophy* (Glasgow: J. Maclehose and Sons, 1903).

SELECT BIBLIOGRAPHY

Sir Francis Galton, *Inquiries into Human Faculty and Its Development* (London: Macmillan, 1883).

Franklin Henry Giddings, *The Principles of Sociology; an Analysis of the Phenomena of Association and of Social Organization* (London and New York: Macmillan, 1896).

Fenton John Anthony Hort, *The Way, the Truth, the Life: the Hulsean Lectures for 1871* (Cambridge and New York: Macmillan, 1893).

Sir James H. Jeans, *Eos: or the Wider Aspects of Cosmogony* (London and New York: K. Paul, Trench, Trubner and Co., Ltd; E. P. Dutton, 1929).

Sir Sidney Colvin, ed., *Letters of John Keats to His Family and Friends* (London and New York: Macmillan and Co., 1891).

Harold Joseph Laski, *Authority in the Modern State* (New Haven: Yale University Press, 1919).

Harold Joseph Laski, *On the Study of Politics an Inaugural Lecture delivered at the London School of Economics and Political Science on 22 October 1926* (London: H. Milford, Oxford University Press, 1926).

John Locke, *Essay on Human Understanding*, ed. A. C. Fraser, 2 vols (Oxford University Press, 1894).

Alfred Firmin Loisy, *La Religion d'Israel* (Paris: E. Nourry, 1917).

Robert M. MacIver, *The Modern State* (Oxford: At the Clarendon Press, 1926).

William McDougall, *An Introduction to Social Psychology* (London: Metheun and Co., 1908).

Hans Morgenthau, *Scientific Man Versus Power Politics* (Chicago: The University of Chicago Press, 1946).

Richard L. Nettleship, *Philosophical Remains of Richard Lewis Nettleship*, ed. with a biographical sketch by A. C. Bradley, 2nd ed. (London and New York: Macmillan, 1901), (originally issued as Volume I of Nettleship's *Philosophical Lectures and Remains*.

Walter Pater, *Plato and Platonism, a series of lectures* (New York and London: Macmillan, 1895).

Josiah Royce, *The Philosophy of Loyalty* (New York: Macmillan, 1908).

George Santayana, *Winds of Doctrine, studies in contemporary opinion* (London: Dent, 1913).

Albert Schweitzer, *Civilization and Ethics, Dale Memorial Lectures 1922* (London: A. and C. Black, Ltd, 1923).

SELECT BIBLIOGRAPHY

Henry Sidgwick, *The Methods of Ethics*, 7th ed. (London and New York: Macmillan, 1907).

Logan Pearsall Smith, *The Prospects of Literature* (London: L. and Virginia Woolf, 1927).

William Ritchie Sorley, *The International Crisis: The Theory of the State; lectures delivered in February and March 1916* (London and New York: H. Milford, Oxford University Press, 1916).

Lionel Spencer Thornton, *Conduct and the Supernatural* (London and New York: Longmans, Green and Co., 1915).

Spinoza, *Epistolae* (Bruder's edition) in: –
    B. de Spinosa Opera quae Supersunt Omnia, ed. by C. H. Bruder (Leipzig (Tauchnitz), 1843). Translation of Spinoza's Correspondence (abridged) in *Philosophy of Benedict Spinoza* of R. H. M. Elwes, 2 vols (London: G. Bell and Son, Bohn's Philosophical Library, 1883).

Spinoza, *Ethica*: –
    First published in 1677 as *Ethica: ordine geometrice demonstrata . . .*, English translation by R. H. M. Elwes in *Philosophy of Benedict Spinoza*, 2 vols (London: G. Bell and Son, Bohn's Philosophical Library, 1883).

Spinoza, *Tractatus*: –
    Tractatus Theologico-Politicus, English translation by R. H. M. Elwes in *Philosophy of Benedict Spinoza*, 2 vols (London: G. Bell and Son, Bohn's Philosophical Library, 1883.

Ernst Troeltsch, *Der Historismus und Seine Probleme* (Tubingen: J. C. B. Mohr, 1922).

Wilhelm Windelband, *An Introduction to Philosophy* (transl. by Joseph McCabe) (London: T. F. Unwin Ltd, 1921), (second impression 1923).

Wittgenstein, *Tractatus*: –
    Ludwig Wittgenstein, *Tractatus-Logico-Philosophicus*, First German edition in *Annalen der Naturphilosophie*, 1921. First English edition (London: Routledge and Kegan Paul Ltd, 1922), with Introduction by Bertrand Russell (International Library of Psychology, Philosophy and Scientific Method).

EDITOR'S ACKNOWLEDGEMENTS

The chance to converse with Michael Oakeshott over a period of sixteen years from 1974 to 1990 was a great blessing. I am further blessed by the dialectical companionship of colleagues and students, only a few of whom I can mention here, in the Oakeshottian engagement to think philosophically about politics.

I owe a special debt, as do all who care about Oakeshott's work, to the proprietor of the Oakeshott papers, the late Shirley Letwin, a dear friend and collaborator for many years. I am grateful also to Kenneth Minogue, Robert Orr and William Letwin, and the sadly departed Elie Kedourie. Christel Oakeshott's hospitality has made the work of retrieving the Oakeshott papers an easier task than it might have been. Former students, now gratifyingly successful colleagues, who, among my many fine students, have particularly assisted me at different stages of my work on Oakeshott are Paul Franco, David Mapel, Judy Swanson and Inger Thomsen. Richard Friedman and Horst Mewes, my longest-standing colleagues in political philosophy, have commented on most of what I have thought or written on any subject, and especially on this one Marianna. McJimsey, not for the first time has created an excellent index.

I must also express my thanks to Colorado College for numerous travel grants that made feasible this work, and much that preceded it.

'Religion and the Moral Life' (The 'D' Society Pamphlets, no. 2, 1927), was first published by Bowes & Bowes in Cambridge, England.

'The Importance of the Historical Element in Christianity' first appeared in *Modern Churchman*, 18 (1928–9), pp. 360–71.

'The Authority of the State' first appeared in *Modern Churchman*, 19 (1929–30), pp. 313–27.

'The Claims of Politics' first appeared in *Scrutiny*, 8 (1939–40), pp. 146–51.

'Scientific Politics' first appeared in *Cambridge Journal*, 1 (1947–8), pp. 347–58.

'The Customer is Never Wrong' first appeared in *The Listener*, 54 (1955), pp. 301–2.

INDEX

Abstractions, 11, 12, 45, 66, 78, 83, 85, 87, 88, 90, 99, 100, 103, 106, 107, 114, 117, 128, 131, 134
Accomplishment, 32, 36
Action, moral, 6, 43, 51;
    political, 81, 82, 93, 94, 145, 151.
Administration, governmental, 101
Affairs, public, 112
Africa, 145
Afterlife, 2
Age, Apostolic, 45;
    New, 28.
America, 22, 109, 111, 117
Anti-nomianism, 20
Antiquarianism, 31
Aquinas, Thomas, 151, 155
Arendt, Hannah, 10 n.
Argentina, 114
Aristotelity, 21
Aristotle, vii n., viii, 10, 19, 48, 57, 58, 59, 117
Arnold, Matthew, 1
Art, 9, 34, 92, 95, 96, 108
Assent, 12
Association, civil, 12 n., 13 n., 26
Athens, 142
Atonement, 64
Attitude, sacramental, 18
Augustine, see St Augustine
Authority, 11, 12, 13, 19, 21, 42;
    claims of, 77;
    Church, 16;
    exercise of, 77;
    legislative, 85, 86;
    of state, 85, 87;
    nature of, 75, 79.
Autonomy, 44

Bacon, Francis, 141
Balfour, Arthur James, 57
Beings, moral, 10

Belief, cause of, 76, 78;
    in science, 98, 99;
    liberal democratic, 112;
    object of, 14, 17, 42, 71, 73;
    religious, 5, 15, 16, 40, 41, 67;
    system, 30.
Beman, 88
Bentham, Jeremy, 50, 51, 101
Bergson, Henri, 121
Bill of Rights, 93
Biology, 47, 48, 57, 58
Bolingbroke, (Henry St John), 72
Bosanquet, Bernard, 5, 41, 60, 88, 89, 90
Bourbons, 31
Boys-Smith, John Sandwith, 4 n.
Bradley, F. H., 25 n., 41
Bultmann, Rudolf, 4 n., 15
Burke, Edmund, 56
Butler, Joseph, 51
Byron, George Gordon, 55

Cambridge, 4, 4 n., 90
Caritas, 10
Career, 31, 33, 34, 35, 36, 37
Catlin, G. E. G., 88
Change, 14, 15, 16, 17, 18, 65, 67, 136, 145, 154, 155
Charity, 108
Charmides, 25 n.
Choice, conduct of life, 2;
    human, 117;
    moral, 6.
Christ, 17, 20, 40, 43, 72
Christianity, 1, 14, 15, 18, 19, 41, 42, 44, 48 n., 57;
    anti-Christian, 20;
    cloistered, 27;
    historical element, 17, 18, 63, 66, 67;
    Hobbes, 20;

INDEX

identity, 67, 68, 73;
　medieval, 2;
　morality and, 45;
　original experience, 2, 64, 65, 67;
　reformed, 16.
Christians, early, 27, 28, 31;
　medieval, 29;
　primitive, 29, 30, 36.
Church, 5, 9, 16, 85, 92;
　of England, 4 n.;
　primitive, 1, 16.
Cicero, 142
Civilization, 26, 29, 45, 93, 95
Clarence, Duke of, 76
Coercion, 77
Coleridge, Samuel Taylor, 61
Common, The, 11
Communism, 23, 102
Community, 12, 22, 42, 56, 58, 82, 83,
　88
Comte, Auguste, 39
Concepts, attributes of, 129, 130;
　nature of, 127;
　valuation, 132, 133.
Condition, human, 8, 14, 18, 19, 20
Conduct, 51;
　moral, 5, 6, 7;
　human, 145;
　of life, 2, 3;
　proper, 21.
Conflict, moral, 104
Conscience, 36
Consciousness, of society, 95;
　religious, 71, 72.
Consent, 13, 86
Content, moral, 6
Continuity, 11
Conversation, 116
Corfu, 55
Cornell University, 88
Corruption, 115
Cowardice, 35
Culture, Greek, 69
Custom, 9, 93

Dante, Alighieri, 53, 56, 82
Day of the Lord, 28
Definition, philosophical, 127, 128, 130
Deists, 59
Democracy, 109;
　liberal, 111, 112, 116, 117, 118
Demagogue, 115
De Monarchia, 82
Demythologization, 4 n.
Dependence, 43

Descartes, René, 142
Dialogues, vii n.
Dichotomy, 30;
　Christianity, 1, 2;
　medieval, 29.
Discoveries, 7 n.
Discourse, community of, 10
Disraeli, Benjamin, 107
Divina Comedia, 56
Doctrine, ethical, 122;
　metaphysical, 122;
　of government, 117;
　philosophical, 128;
　political, 147, 148, 149, 150.
Dogberry, 118
Dogma, 18
D Society, 4, 4 n., 39 n.
Dualism, 28, 30;
　Christian, 20
Duality, 8, 18
Duty, political, 92

Economics, 101
Eddington, 106
Education, 110
Egoism, 103, 104, 106
Electorate, 112
Ely Cathedral, 4 n.
End, The, 28, 30, 31, 33
Engineering, social, 100, 102, 105, 106,
　107
England, 82, 109, 139, 140
Enquiry, rational, 99, 100;
　scientific, 99, 100, 105
Epictetus, 54, 58
Equality, 131
Erasmus, Desiderius, 90
Eschaton, 1
Eternal, The, 18
Ethics, 150
Ethical societies, 39
Europe, 12 n., 26, 72, 73, 97, 98, 100,
　102, 105, 107, 109, 113
Euthyprho, 6
Evil, 39, 50, 104, 105, 107
Experience, Christian, 2, 13, 14, 15;
　common, 117;
　historical, 7;
　human, 4, 6, 8, 22, 40, 126;
　nature of, 23, 139;
　political, 8, 144, 153;
　present, 32, 72;
　religious, 3, 6, 7, 8, 14, 17, 18,
　19.
Experiment, moral, 3, 35

INDEX

Fascism, 102, 147
Facts, 14 n., 88, 141, 152;
    of political life, 123, 124, 126.
Faith, 16, 17, 20, 21;
    politics of, vii;
    rationalist, 101, 102.
Faust, 32
Feelings, 71
Felicity, 21
Feudalism, 147, 148
Fichte, Johann Gottlieb, 52
First Coming, 20
Fleet Street, 55
Founder, 17
France, Anatole, 58
Freedom, 37, 72
Friendship, 10, 55, 57, 58, 59, 60
Future, 33, 34, 35, 36;
    putative, 3.

Galton, Francis, 48
Gellius, Lucius, 142
Germany, 102, 114
Giges und sein Ring, 52
God, 124
    dependence on, 6, 19, 43
    power and, 105;
    reason and, 60;
    relationship with, 5, 7, 39, 40, 41;
    service of, 9, 92;
    sociality and, 59;
    state and, 82;
    will of, 41, 42, 43.
Golden rule, 21
Good, 41, 42, 57, 59, 104, 132;
    highest, 20, 35, 44, 60;
    social, 10.
Goodness, 5, 6, 7
Good Time Coming, 36
Gospels, 28, 42, 43
Government, 13, 82, 83, 85;
    administration of, 101;
    doctrine of, 117;
    liberal democratic, 112, 113, 114,
    115;
    parliamentary, 102, 108, 109;
    theory vs. practice, 117.
Grace, doctrine of, 5, 40
Greenwich Park, 55
Grotius, 101
Ground, logical, 89

Hamlet, 118
Happiness, 51, 125
Hebbel, Friedrich, 52

Hebrew, 28
Hegel, Georg Wilhelm Friedrich, 47, 88,
    89, 90, 126, 135, 137, 150
Heresy, 16
Heroic, The, 10 n.
Historical, The, 17
History, 14 n., 15, 30, 31, 36, 78, 139,
    140;
    belief in, 69, 72;
    Christian, 66;
    education, 110;
    evidence, 140, 141;
    prima facie historical, 64, 66, 68, 69,
    70, 72, 73;
    process of, 65.
Hobbes, Thomas, vii, viii, 8, 9, 13, 16,
    19, 20, 21, 103, 119, 126, 133, 137,
    150, 155.
Housman, A. E., 54
Human, condition, 8, 14, 18, 19;
    relationships, 7.
Hume, David, 117, 138
Hypotheses, 130

Ideas,
    authority of, 79;
    Christian, 29;
    philosophical, 68;
    religious, 17, 68.
Identity, of Christianity, 15, 16, 66, 67,
    68, 73;
    theory of, 65, 66, 68.
Idolatry, 17, 18, 71, 73
Ignorance, 144
Imagination, life of, 54
Immediate, The, 17
Immortality, 32, 37, 71
Incarnation, 17
Independence, 43
Individual, 10, 11, 12, 51
Insight, 33, 34, 37, 38, 43, 44
Intellectual, 14
Interests, communal, 94, 95
Intimations, vii n., 7, 24
Italy, 114

Jacobinism, 113, 115, 116
James, William, 49, 111 n.
Jeans, James H., 32 n.
Jesus, 16, 43, 65
John, *see* St John
Johnson, Samuel, 55
Journalists, 114
Judaism, 69, 73

INDEX

Judgement, 78, 79, 125, 146;
 categorical, 130;
 moral, 136.
Judith, 52
Justice, 10, 57, 59, 108

Kant, Immanuel, 124
Keats, John, 60
Kelsen, Hans, 131
Kerygma, 15
Kierkegaard, Soren, 1
Knowledge, 20, 138, 142, 152;
 historical, 14, 142;
 ordinary, 107, 128;
 scientific, 141.

Lake Victoria, 145
Lamb, Charles, 54
Laplace, 124
Law, 9, 13 n., 21, 26, 52, 85, 86, 93, 131;
 common, 109;
 moral, 41, 42, 43;
 natural, 111 n., 113, 115, 117;
 Roman, 58.
Leaders, 115
Legislation, 108
Letters on History, 72
Leviathan, vii, 13, 20, 21, 119, 150
Liberalism, 100, 102, 107, 108, 109
Liberty, 131
Liddington, John, 4 n.
Life, Christian, 45;
 communal, 93;
 daily, 19, 107;
 good, 46, 50, 56, 113;
 irreligious, 34;
 moral, 5, 41, 44, 45, 50;
 ordinary, 71, 123, 128;
 political, 120, 123, 137;
 public, 9, 92;
 practical, 128;
 religious, 3, 7, 22, 35;
 social, 5, 6, 9, 11, 12;
 unified, 58;
 whole, 58;
 worldly, 3, 7;
 worth, 33.
Life and Liberty group, 88
Lippman, Walter, 22, 23, 111–18
Little Gidding, 17
Liturgy, 18
Locke, John, 9, 16, 65, 86
Love, 57, 58, 59, 60, 71
Loyalty, 57
Lutheran, 21 n.

Magna Carta, 93
Maine, Henry, 118
Man, nature, 48;
 political, 84;
 religious, 2, 3, 34, 36, 37, 38;
 scientific, 105;
 secular, 84;
 worldly, 2, 8, 30, 31, 34.
Marmsey, 76
Masses (of people), 112, 113, 114
Meal, 57
Meaning, 19
Medieval period, 1, 2
Mercantilism, 147
Middle Ages, 28, 45, 109, 148
Mill, John Stuart, 50, 51, 99, 117
Milton, John, 117
Mind, unity of, 58
Modernists, theological, 4 n.
Moloch, 31,
Montaigne, 7 n., 86, 117
Moralism, 23
Morality, 41;
 Christian, 45;
 nature of, 42, 43, 61;
 religion and, 4, 5, 6, 39.
Morgenthau, Hans, 22, 23, 97–110
Mortality, 7
Mundane, The, 10
Mystery, 18
Myth, 15

Natural, 20, 21, 29
Nature, 7, 47, 55;
 man's, 48, 105.
Need, spiritual, 72
Nettleship, Richard L. 55
New, The, 36, 72;
 in philosophy, 129.
New Testament, 65
New Republic, 111 n.
Nicomachean Ethics, vii n.
Nietzsche, 1

Obligation, moral, 52, 104;
 political, 91, 92.
Oman, John Wood, 40, 40 n., 43, 44
Opinion, moral, 86;
 political, 86;
 public, 112, 114, 115, 116.
Order, legal, 9;
 moral, 10;
 present, 30, 31;
 social, 9.

INDEX

Orthodoxy, 16
Owen Falls, 145

Parekh, Bikhu, 4 n.
Parliament, 140, 141
Pascal, Blaise, 41, 74
Past, 33, 34, 35, 36, 72
Pater, Walter, 1
Patriotism, 60, 61
Paul, *see* St Paul
Peace, 112, 114;
    science of, 101.
Pelagius, 103
Pelagianism, 20, 105;
    anti-Pelagianism, 22, 103.
People, ordinary, 14, 17, 71;
    consent of the, 86.
Perfection, 108, 109, 116
Personality, moral, 5, 6, 40, 43, 44
Persons, moral, 5
Phaedrus, 53
Philosophers, 9, 20, 95
Philosophy, aesthetic, 25 n.;
    history of, 50;
    idealistic, 121, 131;
    Jacobin, 115;
    modern, 52;
    moral, 25 n.;
    nature of, 19, 24, 127;
    of religion, 25 n.;
    political, 59, 119, 120, 121, 122;
    politics and, 22, 23, 25, 25 n.;
    public, 22, 113;
    Socratic, 23;
    truth and, 68.
Philosophy of Right, 137, 150
Piety, 6
Planning, social, 109
Plato, vii n., viii, 6, 10, 25 n., 46, 57, 58,
    59, 60, 150, 151, 155
Plotinus, 62
Plutarch, 59
Poets, 9, 96
Policy, public, 112, 145, 147, 150, 154
Politicians, 114, 115
Politics, 8, 9, 10, 20;
    American, 22;
    ideological, 103;
    interest group, 23;
    modern, 97, 98, 100;
    nature of, 93, 105, 107, 146;
    philosophy and, 22, 23, 24, 25;
    philosophy of, 119–137;
    rationalist, 98, 102, 106, 107, 110;
    science of, 100, 106, 109;
    scientific, 108;
    success in, 98;
    theory of, 80;
    world of, 92.
Politics, vii
Portugal, 114
Positivism, 39, 142
Post-medieval period, 1
Power, 87, 103, 104, 105;
    limits on, 109;
    of the masses, 112.
Practicality, of religion, 19
Pragmatism, 121
Prejudice, moral, 3, 35
Present, 3, 33, 34, 36
Preservation, 18
Problems, social, 98
Property, 115
Psychology, 48, 52
Punishment, 135
Puritan, 117
Purity, historical, 19

Rationalism,
    in politics, vii n., 15 n., 22, 23, 99,
        100, 102, 105, 106, 108;
    nature of, 98, 99, 105.
Rationality, 105
Reason, 75, 78, 79;
    life of, 60;
    power of, 98, 105.
Reconciliation, 19
Reflection, 24, 138, 139, 140, 142, 143,
    144, 146, 148, 149, 150, 153, 154.
Reformation, 65
Relations, international, 101
Relationships, human, 7, 11, 145;
    moral, 7, 12.
Religion, 1, 15, 16, 17, 27, 30, 36, 57, 59;
    civil, 22;
    cloistered, 27;
    definition, 3, 34, 42;
    morality and, 4, 5, 39, 42;
    nature of, 3, 19, 34, 37, 42, 67, 68,
        71;
    philosophy of, 25 n.;
    science and, 32 n.
Religion civile, 59
Religious, The, 10
Renaissance, 65
Renan, 40
Republic, viii, 150, 155
Responsibility, political, 9
Restraint, 12
Resurrection, 20

164

INDEX

Revelation, 18, 19
Rickert, 72
Right, 124
Ritual, 18, 71, 73
Rousseau, Jean Jacques, 59, 87, 125
Russia, 114

Sacrament, 18, 71, 72, 73
Sacramentalism, Catholic, 15
St Bernard, 47
St Augustine, 4, 11, 13, 21, 22, 40, 103, 145, 151
St James, 27
St John, 46, 56
St Paul, 10, 28, 58, 60
St Patrick, 140
Salvation, 21, 21 n.
Sanction, moral, 52
Santayana, George, 111 n.
Satisfaction, of complete persons, 84, 85, 87;
    philosophical, 19;
    religious, 19.
Scepticism, vii n.;
    politics of, vii.
Scholasticism, 19
Science, 22, 32 n., 98, 128, 142
Scientism, 22, 23;
    in politics, 105;
    nature of, 98, 99.
Scripture, 78
Second Coming, 20, 28
Secularism, 29, 30, 36
Self, 52, 53, 104
Self-awareness, 6
Selfishness, 104
Self-realization, 32, 125, 134
Self-understanding, 2, 3, 6, 8, 10, 11, 15, 19, 21, 24
Seneca, 117
Sensibility, 34, 35, 37, 44, 73
Service, public, 9;
    social, 92.
Shakespeare, William, 117
Sidgwick, Henry, 51
Simmias, 75
Sisyphus, 32
Sociableness, 47, 53, 54
Sociality, 10, 46, 46 n., 47, 48, 49, 53, 58
Society, 47, 49, 55, 95;
    nature of, 50, 57;
    of men, 55;
    of nature, 55;
    political, 84;
    science of, 106;

utilitarian, 47.
Sociology, 106, 108
Socrates, 23, 25 n., 53, 59, 75, 130
Solitude, 10, 53, 54, 56
Solon, 53
Soul, 29, 53, 57
Sovereign, 21
Spain, 114
Speech, freedom of, 115, 116, 117
Spinoza, Baruch, vii n., viii, 46, 55, 60, 150
Spirit, Christian, 21
State, 11, 12, 131;
    European, 12 n.,
    legal conception, 81, 82;
    nature of, 13;
    patriotism, 60, 61.
Statesman, 107
Strauss, Leo, 10 n., 25 n.
Structure, moral, 6
Struggle, 11
Substance, identity of, 66
Subversion, 24, 140, 141, 142, 147, 148, 149, 150, 154, 155
Summum bonum, 20, 21
Supernatural, 7, 20, 21, 29
Survival, individual, 104
Swift, Jonathan, 34
Syndicalism, 148
System, political, 9, 93

Teleology, 7, 19, 20
Temporality, 4, 14, 18
Theology, 4, 9, 14, 17;
    Christian, 28, 40, 65;
    Hobbes, 20.
Things, 141
Tower of Babel, 3, 8, 15 n.
Tradition, 9, 31, 36, 93;
    Christian, 15, 16, 67, 70;
    political, 110;
    religious, 64;
    scholastic, 21.
Tragedy, 108
Transcendence, 6, 10 n.
Transformation, 133, 134, 135, 142
Truth, 19, 25 n., 68, 75, 116, 122;
    moral, 116;
    necessary, 17;
    of things, 141;
    of opinions, 141;
    political, 116.
Tyranny, 109

Uniqueness, principle of, 72

INDEX

United Nations, 101
Unity, 5, 8, 10, 52, 53, 54, 79, 129;
    of life, 2;
    of mind, 57, 60;
    social, 57, 58.
Utilitarianism, 47, 50, 51, 52, 57

Valuation, 132, 133, 134
Values, intellectual, 1;
    materialistic, 1, 30;
    of society, 95;
    scale of, 30;
    spiritual, 1, 30;
    standard of, 31, 32;
    vulgar, 1.
Versailles, 111 n.
Voltaire, 48
Vulgarity, 93

Wagner, Richard, 32
Ward, Lester, 108
Welfare, social, 109
West, The, 23, 117
Will, general, 123, 136
    of God, 41, 42, 43.
Wilson, Woodrow, 111 n.

Wisdom, 44
Whole, 25 n., 79;
    nature of, 12;
    political, 82, 84;
    secular, 82, 84;
    social, 9, 10, 22, 51, 57, 83, 84, 88, 93.
Wordsworth, William, 54, 55
Works, 21
World, 5, 21, 27;
    human, 1;
    material, 2, 28, 29, 30;
    moral, 39;
    natural, 2, 30, 98;
    of flesh, 1;
    of spirit, 1;
    of thought, 1;
    political, 10;
    secular, 28;
    social, 98, 99, 106;
    spiritual, 28, 29, 30;
    supernatural, 2;
    Western, 117.
Worldly, the, 10, 22
World War II, 9, 22, 111 n.

Youth, 33, 34, 35, 36, 38